do-it-yourself agility equipment

Constructing Agility Obstacles for Training or Competition

by Jim Hutchins

Clean Run Productions LLC

Do-It-Yourself Agility Equipment: Constructing Agility Obstacles for Training or Competition

For information contact:
Clean Run Productions, LLC
35 N. Chicopee St., Chicopee, MA 01020
Phone: 413-532-1389 or 800-311-6503
Fax: 413-532-1590
Website: www.cleanrun.com

Book design and typesetting by DDGraphix, www.ddgraphix.com

Cover design by DDGraphix

Cover photo by JT pawPrints, www.jtpawprints.com

Equipment photos by Jim Hutchins

Illustrations by Jim Hutchins, Linda Mecklenburg, and Monica Percival

Drafting for A-frame and dogwalk welding plans by Bill Haefele

Editing by Lisa Baird, Nini Bloch, Linda Mecklenburg, Monica Percival, and Marcille Ripperton

Printing by Hadley Printing Company, Inc.

Trademarks: All service marks, trademarks, and product names used in this publication belong to their respective holders.

First edition

First printing November 2002

ISBN 1-892694-00-X

Disclaimer

All drawings within have been published by Clean Run Productions ("Clean Run"), have been prepared by and are the property of HOGA Agility ("HOGA"), and are provided to the customer "as-is." These drawings were not prepared or checked by a licensed engineer or architect. HOGA does not represent or imply itself to be licensed architects or engineers. These drawings cannot be reproduced without consent.

Dog agility is an inherently dangerous sport for you and your dog. HOGA has made every effort to ensure that equipment built according to these plans, if constructed properly and used with common sense, will make sturdy and safe obstacles. However, since neither HOGA nor Clean Run can control the individual use of HOGA's plans, the construction techniques of the individual consumer, or the site conditions where the equipment will be used, neither HOGA nor Clean Run Productions is responsible for any accidents or injuries or other incidental, special, consequential, or indirect damages of any kind resulting from the customer's use of these plans. In any case, HOGA and Clean Run's liability to you or any third party shall not exceed the price paid for this product.

Similarly, power tools are inherently dangerous and many of the solvents, cleaners, and adhesives described in these plans are dangerous if inhaled or otherwise used improperly. Accordingly, you should always follow the individual manufacturer's instructions provided with tools, solvents, adhesives, and paints purchased from third parties. The manufacturer's instructions that come with such tools and materials always supersede HOGA's instructions.

dedication

This book is dedicated to Kiri, the greatest dog who never did agility.

about the author

Mike Godsil, Godsil Photography

Jim Hutchins has been active in agility training since 1994. During that time, he has had only two agility partners, Annie and Dylan, both Australian Cattle Dogs. Jim and Annie are currently competing at the Excellent level in AKC agility and at the Masters/PIII level in USDAA agility. Annie is also an AKC Obedience Companion Dog Excellent. Dylan is a part-time partner who primarily runs with Jim's wife, Rosemary Hoffman.

Jim has worked as ring crew at the 1995 USDAA Grand Prix and at the 1996 and 1997 AKC Nationals. As an example of his equipment problem-solving skills, he was instrumental in modifying a seesaw that was too tall for the 1996 AKC Nationals: using a pickaxe, he dug a hole in the hardpacked dirt of the Lazy E Arena in Guthrie, Oklahoma to reduce the height of the seesaw by 2".

Outside of agility, Jim is Associate Professor of Anatomy at the University of Mississippi Medical Center, teaching brain structure and function to first-year medical and dental students. He has been named an "All-Star" teacher twice by the medical students and was named "Basic Science Professor of the Year" by the medical students in 2002 and by the dental students in 2001.

Jim and Rosemary teach Basic Home Manners classes to dogs and their owners in the Jackson, Mississippi metropolitan area (www.MissDogManners.com).

Teaching has given Jim experience in breaking down difficult procedures into simple, clear steps.

table of contents

*i*ntroduction

You can't make everything yourself. And, even if you could, you might not want to. I estimate that a complete set of equipment, suitable for running a sanctioned AKC, NADAC, or USDAA trial, would cost $5,000 to $6,000 if you buy it and maybe one-third to one-half of that if you build it yourself using these plans. It's almost half again as much (about $3,000), if you plan on doing more than one form of agility; differences in the obstacle specifications from organization to organization force clubs to have more than one version of some obstacles. If you are equipment manager for your club, expect a lot of work. You will die a little bit inside every time you see someone moving equipment. Learn to accept the inevitable wear and tear on club equipment. Keep a lot of extra jump cups around—they break (if plastic) or break off (if metal)—and plenty of paint for touch-ups before a big event.

If you're just building backyard equipment for training your own dogs, it's much easier. You don't have to worry about interpreting those cryptic equipment specifications, and you can keep around just what you like. For my individual training, I try to build obstacles that are as "difficult" as I might ever see in trials. For example, I build the weave poles so that the spacing between poles is as tight as is legal; I make the chute as small as is legal; and I make the seesaw as high and noisy as is legal.

You can get steel welding done pretty easily, but a good aluminum welder is very hard to find. You might want to consider just buying things like metal dogwalk bases. (I really like the MAX 200/Pipe Dreams adjustable dogwalk bases, even though they're expensive.) But, if you want to do your own or have them made by a welder, there are plans in this book.

When you go to agility trials, use the time in between runs to look at what other people have made and try to figure out how they did it. There are some really creative and skilled people out there and a wealth of good ideas for equipment building.

Guidelines for Building Obstacles

The information in this section is intended to be a reference guide for all of the construction plans included in this book. It's a good idea to read it through once before you get started on your first building project.

Selecting PVC Pipe and Fittings

A number of the plans in this book call for PVC pipe and fittings. Although you can use the schedule 40 PVC plumbing pipe that is readily available from home stores and hardware stores for all of the plans, in the long run, you may be happier with furniture-grade PVC pipe and fittings. Although furniture-grade pipe and fittings are more expensive than schedule 40 pipe and fittings, they are also higher quality and last longer. Here are some of the other benefits:

- Ultraviolet light resistant—important if you intend to leave your equipment outdoors exposed to the elements and you want it to last many years without becoming cracked or brittle.

- High-impact resistant—important if you toss your equipment around and move it a lot.

- High-gloss finish—important if you like your equipment to look nice.

- Custom colors—important if you like to customize the look of your equipment.

- Ease of use—the finish of the pipe makes it easy to work with, and there's less splitting when you cut and drill it.

- Less variation in fittings—there are so many manufacturers of plumbing PVC parts that there is a lot of variation in the sizes of the fittings, which forces you to adjust measurements or search several hardware stores to find parts that are all exactly the same. This is much less likely to be a problem with furniture-grade parts.

- Special fittings available—there are several specialty parts (such as 5-way tees) that are great for making agility equipment that are not available in a schedule 40 version.

- No cleaning required—schedule 40 PVC is usually pretty dirty (even right off the shelves) and has writing printed on it. If you want it to look nice, you need to clean it. Even if you're not a neatnik, at the very least, you need to get the gritty dirt off schedule 40 PVC pipe so that the parts fit together properly and can be glued.

If you would like to try furniture-grade PVC pipe and parts, several vendors are listed in the "Resource Guide."

If you prefer to use schedule 40 plumbing PVC, you may want to clean off the writing as described below.

Cleaning PVC Pipe

For anything made from schedule 40 PVC pipe, you can create a nicer-looking finished product if you clean the writing off the pipe with acetone. Acetone is available in the paint supplies section of the hardware store. It is a flammable solvent and should be used with extreme caution: it is absorbed through the skin and it's potentially harmful to inhale. However, if you use appropriate gloves and work in a well-ventilated area far away from open flames like pilot lights on gas heaters, it's great for removing the ugly writing off the PVC pipe you buy at the hardware or home store. Just be sure to follow the product directions and warnings.

1. Wearing gloves, soak a rag with acetone.

2. Rub the rag vigorously over the writing on the pipe. It will take a little time and a little elbow grease, but the writing will come off. It helps to keep using a fresh part of the rag. I find that some inks can be removed completely, while others are almost impossible to completely remove.

3. The PVC will be gummy for a few seconds so either find a clean place to lay it down or stand there like a fool for about 30 seconds waiting for it to dry.

Cutting PVC Pipe

Be sure to wear protective gear when you are cutting PVC pipe and fittings. Even if you're being very careful with your cuts, it's not unusual for pieces of plastic to chip off and become flying projectiles that can cut you or someone else.

Gluing PVC Pipe and Parts

When working with PVC cement, work in an area with adequate ventilation. This stuff is nasty and can cause health problems. Check the can for particulars.

Before you glue PVC pipe and parts together, you should "dry fit" all of the pieces to make sure everything fits together perfectly. Because of differences in the fittings sold by different manufacturers, you'll find that it's sometimes necessary to trim a little PVC here or there or even to cut a new piece because a pipe needs to be slightly longer. Better to find this out before you glue as there's no going back—PVC cement dries very quickly and even if you do manage to pry pieces apart, the residual glue makes it nearly impossible to reglue them.

Always work with your test assemblies on a flat surface so that you can make sure that all the parts lie flat and there's no warping or bowing.

If you are gluing together assemblies where some of the fittings have an empty hole, it is often helpful to insert a scrap piece of PVC in those holes so that you have more leverage in making small adjustments to get things lined up just right.

Once I'm happy with the test assembly, I take apart just one section and glue those parts together. When they're set, I take apart the next section and glue those parts, and so on.

1. Take the brush from the can of cement and apply the cement to both surfaces to be joined.

2. Push the two parts together with a twisting motion. Work quickly since the cement sets in about 20 seconds, sometimes much less.

3. Use a rag to wipe off the excess glue around the joint.

Selecting Lumber

It's hard to find good wood at home centers, especially since much of the lumber is intended for projects where it won't be visible (such as studs in a wall). So if you have an old-style, traditional lumberyard in your town, particularly one that caters to carpenters and builders, that's where I would recommend you start looking when plans in this book call for lumber. Carefully inspect the wood for "waniness" (bends or twists in the wood). Pick only the best quality.

Most wooden obstacles that are being built for outdoor use need to be made from pressure-treated lumber. The drawback is that pressure-treated lumber is heavy and somewhat more expensive than untreated. In parts of the country near the seacoast, marine-grade lumber may be available, and that is your best choice if you can get it.

I have not experimented with different types of wood, but I am told that some types of wood are more resistant to water damage and rot than others. You will have to consult with the lumberyard salesperson to get a recommendation for what's best for your area.

Generally, buying "bargain" lumber is not a good idea as no one wants to rebuild equipment every few months. Using higher quality materials is more expensive, but also results in a finished product that lasts much longer.

Painting Wooden Obstacles

No matter how good the lumber you choose, your equipment won't last long outdoors if you don't protect the wood by painting it.

What Color Paint?

I don't care what you were taught, dogs are able to see color. They are, however, red-green colorblind (this is the most common type of color blindness in humans). This means that colors in the red-orange-yellow-green range (including the ones that are paler or less saturated, like pink) are difficult for the dog to tell apart.

You might want to bear this in mind when painting and decorating agility equipment. I once saw dozens of dogs crash a broad jump at a trial. The jump was maroon with white stripes to mark the sides and the trial was being held indoors on sod. Indoors, there is a lot less light (as any photographer knows), so it is more difficult for the dogs to distinguish color and texture. I believe the dogs could not see the jump at all: the maroon center of the broad jump (dark red) would blend perfectly into the grass (dark green).

As far as contact zones go, you are required to use yellow. I don't worry about painting the rest of the equipment in a color that dogs can see against the yellow (such as blue), since I don't personally believe that dogs "see" contacts so much as "feel" whether they are at the end of the board (two feet on the ground and two on the equipment). However, if you're painting obstacles for use in a trial, it's a good idea to select a contrasting color that will make it easy for the judges to see the break between the contact zone and rest of the plank (for example, white is not a good color to paint the rest of the obstacle since it's very hard to distinguish against yellow).

You don't have to agree with me on this!

What Kind of Paint?

Paint comes in two basic types:

- Alkyd—These oil-based paints form a hard, durable finish, but are more expensive and harder to work with—you need to use turpentine or paint thinner to clean up. It's important to be aware that once you paint something with alkyd paint, all subsequent coats have to be alkyd as well.

- Latex—These paints are cheaper and cleanup is a snap.

Regardless of which type of paint you choose, I recommend using disposable paint trays and those disposable mini-rollers that come in 4" or 6" lengths. I reuse paint brushes. I keep a 2" brush around, which is my all-purpose brush.

If you're not really selective about color, you can get paint inexpensively in the "goof" section of your local home center. At the very least, you can use a hideous shade of puce as a primer coat.

Keep looking through the paint samples until you find the bright colors. Basically, no color is too lurid for agility equipment. I've used Lizard Green and Barney Purple to good effect.

Remember that contact zones must be yellow. I like a color identical to, or close to, Traffic Yellow.

Resource Guide

There are a number of companies referenced in these plans and also other companies that sell products or parts useful to the agility equipment builder and the agility enthusiast. I have assembled this contact list for your convenience. Please be aware that this list

- Is by no means inclusive; it's just the businesses that I've heard about or that gave me contact information. There are new sources of agility equipment and accessories cropping up all the time. Use a search engine on the web to look for new ones.

- Is as up-to-date as possible at the time of this printing. However, companies do move and unfortunately sometimes go out of business or discontinue products, so please don't be angry with me if you can't contact someone on the list!

- Is not an endorsement of any of these companies. This is a resource list and I cannot vouch for the business practices of any company on the list. It's up to you to do your homework before ordering.

Agility Obstacles

Action Jack Agility
www.actionjackagility.com

Action K-9 Sports Equipment Co.
27425 Cataluna Cir., Sun City, CA 92585
(909) 679-3699, (909) 679-9309 fax
www.actionk9.com
duncan@actionk9.com

Affordable Agility
PO Box 237, Bloomfield, NY 14469
(585) 229-4936, (585) 229-4010 fax
www.affordableagility.com/home.htm
Pam@AffordableAgility.com

Agilitude
(916) 387-9590
www.agilitudebyheath.com
sales@agilitudebyheath.com

Agility by Carlson
Brad Carlson, 15271 Williamsport Pike,
Greencastle, PA 17225
(717) 597-5076, (717) 597-5150 fax
www.dogtrainingbyh-e.com/agility.htm
bhcar@epix.net

Agility-Equipment.com
Toby and Jim Mazrolle, 6 Cushing Rd.,
Goffstown, NH 03045
(603) 497-5558
www.agility-equipment.com
tailwaggers@attbi.com

Agility for Less
Canandaigua, NY
(585) 749-4808
www.agilityforless.com

Agility Of Course
458 Blakesley-Nurse Hollow Rd.,
Afton, NY 13730
(607) 693-3647, (561) 423-6103 fax
http://members.aol.com/psbdrcolli
psbdrcolli@aol.com

AgilityPro
10246 Hightower, Cincinnati, OH 45249
(512) 530-5057
www.agilitypro.com/main.html
sales@agilitypro.com

AgilityUK
Colin or Jan
 01978 841843
www.agilityuk.com
colin-jan@agilityuk.com

Agility Works
Vacaville, CA
(707) 448-7577
www.agilityworks.com/index.html
info@agilityworks.com

Alfresco Kennels
RR 1, Waterford, ON N0E 1Y0 Canada
(519) 443-6558, (519) 443-4971 fax
www.execulink.com/ ~ alfresco/
Alfresco_Kennx.html

Bow-Wow Video and Agility Equipment
4201 Westgate Ave., Suite A-5, West Palm
Beach, FL 33409
(561) 686-3575, (561) 686-3574 fax
www.bowwowvideo.com
OTCHMACH@aol.com

Canadian Dog Agility Equipment
1240 Mountain View Rd., Armstrong, BC
V0E 1B0, Canada
(250) 546-8416, (250) 546-8492 fax
www.canadiandogagilityequipment.ca
canadiandog@telus.net

Chinookwind Outfitters
PO Box 218, Conifer, CO 80433
(866) 626-1099, (303) 679-9489 fax
www.chinookwind.com
dogsport@chinookwind.com

Durable Versatile Obedience Rally Agility K9' Stuff (DVORAK'S)
Roy Dvorak, 4665 W. 102nd Pl.,
Westminster, CO 80031
(303) 465-2820
www.himmlisch.com/agility.htm
himeldad@aol.com

Foothill Flyers Agility
Terri Swenson, 294 Kilham Rd.,
Auburn, CA 95603
(530) 889-2722
Footflyagility@yahoo.com

Gear To Go, Inc.
PO Box 222683, Hollywood, FL 33022
(954) 929-7117, (954) 929-7046 fax
www.geartogo.net

GEM Agility Equipment
Phoenix, AZ
(602) 439-3993
info@aaadogs.com

Howling Moon Enterprises
291 Ye Olde Canterbury Rd.,
Northwood, NH 03261
(603) 942-5717
www.howlingmoonagility.com
Howlmn@aol.com

Its4Dogs Equipment
3164 Rexland Pl., Murfreesboro, TN 37129
(615) 867-7144 phone and fax
www.its4dogs.com
agiletaz@its4dogs.com

JetSet Agility Equipment
24407 W. 85th Terr., Lenexa, KS 66227
(913) 441-8665, (913) 422-7854 fax
http://members.aol.com/jetsetset/
jetsetagility.htm
jetsetset@aol.com

J and J Dog Supplies, Inc.
PO Box 1517, Galesburg, IL 61402
(800) 642-2050, (309) 344-3522 fax
www.jandjdog.com
info@jandjdog.com

K-9 Agility Equipment
www.k-9agility.com
rick@k-9agility.com

K&S Dog Agility
That General Store
Box 1223, Hebron, OH 43025
(718) 504-6347
www.thatgeneralstore.homestead.com/
agility.html

K.I.S.S. Weave Poles
Sam Turner, 2716 Shadecrest Rd.,
Land O'Lakes, FL 34639
(813) 996-6421
http://members.aol.com/agumbandit/
index1.htm
S1Turner@aol.com

Kit N Kaboodle Agility
Midland, TX
jalynn37@swbell.com

MAD Agility Equipment
390 Summit Rd., McClure, PA 17841
(717) 543-5693
www.madagility.com
madequipt@acsworldnet

MAX 200/Pipe Dreams
114 Beach St., Bldg. 5, Rockaway, NJ 07866
(800) 446-2920, (973) 983-1368 fax
www.max200.com
info@max200.com

Mega-Dogs Displaceable Tires for NADAC
22609 102nd Ave. SE
Woodinville, WA 98072
(425) 487-3078
www.mega-dogs.com
karen@mega-dogs.com

Northwest Agility Products
846 W. Smith Rd., Bellingham, WA 98226
(360) 384-2978
www.nwagility.com
info@nwagility.com

Over! Rover Agility Equipment
1213 Garden St., Ste. N, Titusville, FL 32796
(866) 837-7683, (321) 267-9182 fax
www.overrover.com

PawPrint Agility
852 Havencrest Dr., Las Vegas, NV 89110
http://home.earthlink.net/ ~ heinzman5/final
gsdagility@aol.com

Paw-Z-Tracks Dog Training and Equipment Ltd.
Box 39, Site 1, RR 7, Calgary, AB T2P 2G7,
Canada
(403) 248-8744, (403) 272-4480 fax
www.paw-z-tracks.com
sales@paw-z-tracks.com

Monique Plinck
569 Cook Hill Rd., Cheshire, CT 06410
(203) 699-9961 or (860) 636-7892
Plinckm@aetna.com

Premier Agility Equipment
Triddles Farm, Plough Rd.,
Smallfield Nr Horley, Surrey RH6 9JN
England
01342 842454, 01342 844241 fax
www.premier-agility.nildram.co.uk/
info@premier-agility.co.uk
Export agility equipment from the U.K.

Rewarding Pawsibilities
6369 Eagle Ct., Mason, OH 45040
(513) 398-7922
reward@spectrumanalytic.com

Shadow Hill Shelties Agility Equipment
Pinehurst, NC
(910) 295-3765, (910) 295-4121 fax
www.pinehurst.net/ ~ shelties/
agilityequipment.html
shelties@pinehurst.net

Sondog Agility
Wes or Lois Mierau, Site 206, Box 11, RR 2,
Saskatoon, SK S7K 3J5 Canada
(306) 934-6660
www.sondog.com
sondog@sk.sympatico.ca

Stars & Stripes Agility Training Center
3971 Boyer St., Chino, CA 91710
(909) 590-1170
www.starsandstripesagility.com
sasagility@msn.com

Summit Peak Performance Products
Kristin Boucher, 5 Windham Rd.,
Marlborough, CT 06447
www.summitagility.com
herdingrot@aol.com

Teeters and Weaves
Jim Lizius, Mesa, AZ
www.mindspring.com/~jliziu/
agilitytools.html

Texas 2-Step Agility Equipment
207 S. Elm St., Brady, TX 76825
(915) 243-5397
www.tx2stepagility.com

The Agility Connection
9227 N Kenwood Ave., Kansas City,
MO 64155
(816) 734-9892
www.theagilityconnection.com
skihusky@aol.com

The Agility Zone
5320 Oaks Landing Ct., Buford, GA 30518
www.agilityzone.com
info@agilityzone.com

Collapsed Tunnel Parts & Accessories

Commercially-Available Chutes
Dog Dreams
(877) 998-1088
dogdream@ix.netcom.com

EEZI Crate Manufacturing
4270 Jamie Ln., Conway, SC 29527
(843) 365-9798
www.eezi-crate.com
Chutes for practice tunnels

J&J Dog Supplies
PO Box 1517, Galesburg, IL 61402
(800) 642-2050, (309) 344-3522 fax
www.jandjdog.com
info@jandjdog.com

Nancy Lindsay
(815) 485-9180
herdnk9@aol.com

MAX 200/Pipe Dreams
114 Beach St., Bldg. 5, Rockaway, NJ 07866
(800) 446-2920, (973) 983-1368 fax
www.max200.com
info@max200.com

Texas Canvas Products
(972) 790-1501

Wasatch Agility
123 W. Golden Harvest Rd.,
Draper, UT 84020
(801) 571-8061
www.wasatchagility.com
chawk@networld.com

Fabric for Making Chutes
Beacon Fabric & Notions
6801 Gulfport Bvld. S., Ste. 10,
South Pasadena, FL 33707
(800) 713-8157, (800) 707-3765 fax
www.beaconfabric.com

Hang-Em High Fabrics
1420 Yale Ave., Richmond, VA 23224
(804) 233-6155
www.citystar.com/hang-em-high

Seattle Fabrics
8702 Aurora Ave. N., Seattle, WA
(206) 525-0670
www.seattlefabrics.com

Textile Outfitters
735 10th Ave. SW, Calgary, AB T2R 0B3
Canada
(403) 543-7676, (403) 543-7677 fax
www.justmakeit.com/fabrics/utility/
uc_ripstop.html
moreinfo@justmakeit.com

Plastic Barrels
Global Equipment Company
(800) 645-1232
www.globalindustrial.com

U.S. Plastics
Lima, OH
(800) 537-9724
www.usplastic.com

Fence Posts
Jeffers Equine
PO Box 100, Dothan, AL 36302
(800) 533-3377
www.jefferslivestock.com
Stick-in-the-ground fence posts can be used as marker poles or weave poles

Furniture-Grade PVC Pipe & Parts
A to Z Supply
13396 Ridge Rd., Grass Valley, CA 95945
(530) 273-6608
www.atozsupply.com
sales@atozsupply.com

Patios To Go
307 N. Highway 27, Clermont, FL 34711
(352) 243-3220, (352) 243-3221 fax
www.patiostogo.com

PenBay Ace Hardware/The PVC Store
403 Wilson St., Brewer, ME 04412
(866) 423-7473, (207) 989-1003 fax
www.acepvc.com
gryghost@midmaine.com
Currently available colors of 1 ¼" pipe are red, yellow, pink, and blue. They will also cut pipe to your specifications.

The PVC Store
www.thepvcstore.com
Dealers nationwide

U.S. Plastics
Lima, OH
(800) 537-9724
www.usplastic.com

Hard-to-Find Hardware
Grainger
www.grainger.com/Grainger/locator.jsp
Locations nationwide

McMaster Carr
Atlanta (404) 346-7000
Chicago (630) 833-0300
Cleveland (330) 995-5500
Los Angeles (562) 692-5911
New Jersey (732) 329-3200
www.mcmaster.com

Small Parts Inc.
PO Box 4650, Miami Lakes, FL 33014
(800) 220-4242
www.smallparts.com

Jump Parts & Accessories
Jump Cups
California Agility Supply House
4636 Van Nuys Blvd.
Sherman Oaks, CA 91403
(818) 990-5644, (818) 990-2621 fax

Camp Bandy Pet Resort
9376 Main St., Amherst Jct., WI 54407
(715) 824-3900
www.campbandy.com
laurie@campbandy.com

D and K Agility Equipment
Don or Kim Holmes, 5737 Dennison Rd., Toledo, OH 43615
(419) 531-8006
www.myk9software.com/DANDK
kim.a.holmes@gte.net

Patios To Go
307 N. Highway 27, Clermont, FL 34711
(352) 243-3220, (352) 243-3221 fax
www.patiostogo.com

K9Sports.com, Inc.
PO Box 17643, Encino, CA 91416
(818) 335-9889
www.K9Sports.com
info@k9sports.com

Lee-Perry Belleau
PO Box 276, Marysville, MI 48040
(989) 239-2320
lpbelleau@diamondcs.net

MAX 200/Pipe Dreams
114 Beach St., Bldg. 5, Rockaway, NJ 07866
(800) 446-2920, (973) 983-1368 fax
www.max200.com
info@max200.com

PenBay Ace Hardware/The PVC Store
403 Wilson St., Brewer, ME 04412
(866) 423-7473, (207) 989-1003 fax
www.acepvc.com
gryghost@midmaine.com

Material and Accessories for Making Fabric Wings
Beacon Fabric & Notions
6801 Gulfport Bvld. S., Ste. 10,
South Pasadena, FL 33707
(800) 713-8157, (800) 707-3765 fax
www.beaconfabric.com

Hang-Em High Fabrics
1420 Yale Ave., Richmond, VA 23224
(804) 233-6155
www.citystar.com/hang-em-high

PenBay Ace Hardware/The PVC Store
403 Wilson St., Brewer, ME 04412
(866) 423-7473, (207) 989-1003 fax
www.acepvc.com
gryghost@midmaine.com
Snap-on clamps for attaching banners or
fabric to PVC pipe

Seattle Fabrics
8702 Aurora Ave. N., Seattle, WA
(206) 525-0670
www.seattlefabrics.com

Textile Outfitters
735 10th Ave. SW, Calgary, AB T2R 0B3
Canada
(403) 543-7676, (403) 543-7677 fax
www.justmakeit.com
moreinfo@justmakeit.com

Tape (Colored Vinyl)
Emedco
Buffalo, NY
(800) 442-3633
www.emedco.com/emed2/default.asp

Grainger
www.grainger.com/Grainger/locator.jsp
Locations nationwide

Identi-Tape
83 N. Adams St., Eugene, OR 97402
(877) 917-8273
www.identi-tape.com/index.html
info@identi-tape.com

Industrial Safety Co.
1390 Neubrecht Rd., Lima, OH 45801
(800) 809-4805, (800) 854-5498 fax
www.indlsafety.com

Patios To Go
307 N. Highway 27, Clermont, FL 34711
(352) 243-3220, (352) 243-3221 fax
www.patiostogo.com

Pipe Tunnels & Accessories
Tie-Downs
Cherie's Shades
Cherie Moldenhauer, 200 LF Baum Rd.,
East Helena, MT 59635
(406) 227-0885
www.geocities.com/cheriesshades
Tunnel weights

Clean Run Productions, LLC
35 N. Chicopee St., Chicopee,
MA 01020
(800) 311-6503, (413) 532-1590 fax
www.cleanrun.com
info@cleanrun.com
Tunnel Snuggers

Nelson Industries Ltd.
Box 15, RR 2, Dugald, MB R0E 0K0 Canada
 (204) 444-2457, (204) 444-7822 fax
www.geocities.com/thinkndo.geo/
SaddleBagTunnelHolders.html
djs007@escape.ca
Saddlebag tunnel holders

Tunnels for Practice
Affordable Agility
PO Box 237, Bloomfield, NY 14469
(585) 229-4936, (585) 229-4010 fax
www.affordableagility.com/home.htm
Pam@AffordableAgility.com

Constructive Playthings
13201 Arrington Rd., Grandview, MO 64030
(800) 448-4115

Duck Ware
1-866-K9S-4FUN
www.duckware-stuff.com
duckware@duckware-stuff.com

Flaghouse
(800) 793-7900
www.flaghouse.com

Ikea
(800) 661-9807

Tinker Tots
5770 E. River Valley Trl., Anaheim Hills,
CA 92807
www.tinkertots.com/dogagtraintu.html

Troll Learn and Play
100 Corporate Dr., Mahwah, NJ 07430
(800) 247-6106, (800) 451-0812 fax

Tunnels for Competition
Action K-9 Sports Equipment Co.
27425 Cataluna Cir, Sun City, CA 92585
(909) 679-3699, (909) 679-9309 fax
www.actionk9.com
duncan@actionk9.com

Affordable Agility
PO Box 237, Bloomfield, NY 14469
(585) 229-4936, (585) 229-4010 fax
www.affordableagility.com/home.htm
Pam@AffordableAgility.com

J and J Dog Supplies, Inc.
PO Box 1517, Galesburg, IL 61402
(800) 642-2050, (309) 344-3522 fax
www.jandjdog.com
info@jandjdog.com

K9Sports.com, Inc.
PO Box 17643, Encino, CA 91416
(818) 335-9889
www.k9sports.com
webmaster@k9sports.com

MAX 200/Pipe Dreams
114 Beach St., Bldg. 5, Rockaway, NJ 07866
(800) 446-2920, (973) 983-1368 fax
www.max200.com
info@max200.com

Newmarket Hose House
Michelle Thornhill, 1111 Davis Dr., PO Box
93018, Newmarket, ON L3Y 8K3, Canada
www.dogtube.com
Dogtube@aol.com

Over! Rover Agility Equipment
1213 Garden St., Ste. N, Titusville, FL 32796
(866) 837-7683, (321) 267-9182 fax
www.overrover.com

Rocket Tunnels
Don Soucy, 15 Meadowlark Dr.
Hudson, NH 03051
(603) 883-8652
www.rockettunnels.com
DSoucy1035@aol.com

The Tunnel Man
Don Sawford, RR 22, 6924 Concession 2,
Cambridge, ON, N3C 2V4 Canada
(519) 823-1742, (519) 829-4018 fax
www.thetunnelman.com
dsawford@yahoo.com

Weave Pole Parts & Accessories

Jeffers Equine
PO Box 100, Dothan, AL 36302
(800) 533-3377
www.jefferslivestock.com
Fence posts can be used as stick-in-the-ground weave poles

PenBay Ace Hardware/The PVC Store
403 Wilson St., Brewer, ME 04412
(866) 423-7473, (207) 989-1003 fax
www.acepvc.com
gryghost@midmaine.com
PVC spikes for making weave poles

TuffMutt Agility Equipment
www.tuffmutt.com
info@tuffmutt.com
Weave pole training guide wires

Chapter one

Jumps and Hurdles

gility jumps consist of:

- The center of the jump—One or more displaceable bars, rails, poles, or panels.
- The sides of the jump (called standards)—Vertical uprights with or without "wings." Wing is an equestrian term for a jump upright that has a horizontal extension. Wings are usually about two feet wide. While many wings look like a simple section of fence, they also come in a variety of inventive and decorative shapes and designs; for example, wings could be shaped like dogs or fire hydrants.

There are

- Bar jumps (winged and nonwinged) where the bars or panels are placed one directly above the other.
- Oxers or spread jumps (winged and nonwinged) where the bars are placed across the width of the jump so that the dog has to jump both high and wide. This category includes the double and the triple jumps.

Other types of hurdles used in agility are the

- Tire jump
- Broad or long jump

Jump Heights

- If you are building jumps for competition, you should double-check the regulation jump heights for the appropriate organization(s). Most of the organizations have up-to-date copies of their rulebooks or equipment specifications on their websites. Please be aware that while it doesn't happen often, the jump heights in different organizations have changed several times over the years.

- If you are building jumps for training classes, you may want to attach jump cups every 2" so that you will have a great deal of flexibility for working with dogs of different sizes and ages.

- If you are building jumps for your backyard, you can save money by only attaching jump cups for the heights you use when training your own dogs.

The jump heights used by AKC, NADAC/ASCA, and USDAA at the time of this printing are shown on the following page. This information is provided only as a reference for your convenience. Again, it's always a good idea to check the current rules for changes or updates before committing time and money to building equipment.

AKC Regular Classes

Jump Height	Dog's Height at the Withers
8"	10" and under
12"	14" and under
16"	18" and under
20"	22" and under
24"	Over 22"

USDAA Championship Classes

Jump Height	Dog's Height at the Withers
12"	12" and under
16"	16" and under
22"	21" and under
26"	Over 21"

NADAC/ASCA Regular Classes

Jump Height	Dog's Height at the Withers
8"	11" and under
12"	14" and under
16"	18" and under
20"	20" and under
24"	Over 20" (optional)

AKC Preferred Classes

Jump Height	Dog's Height at the Withers
4"	10" and under
8"	14" and under
12"	18" and under
16"	22" and under
20"	Over 22"

USDAA Performance Classes

Jump Height	Dog's Height at the Withers
8"	12" and under
12"	16" and under
16"	21" and under
22"	Over 21"

NADAC/ASCA Veteran & JH Classes

Jump Height	Dog's Height at the Withers
4"	11" and under
8"	14" and under
12"	18" and under
16"	Over 18"

Measuring the Jump Heights

The height of a jump bar is measured from the ground to the *top* of the bar. For example, 1" schedule 40 PVC (as specified in the regulations) is actually 1 1/4" in diameter. Therefore, the bottom of the jump cups should be 1 1/4" below the actual jump height you want.

To make life easier when building jumps, I keep a 1"-2" piece of PVC around the workshop to use as a test bar. After I mount a jump cup, I put the test bar in the cup to check my math. Use a rubber band or duct tape to keep the test bar in the cup while you are measuring. Be sure that your test bar is the same diameter PVC as you are using for your bars.

Measuring the Jump Width (Spread)

For spread jumps, the width or span of the jump is determined by measuring from the center of the front pole to the center of the back pole (while the bars are parallel). You can measure these distances without using a test bar. Just measure from the center of your jump cups.

Jump Cups

You will need two jump cups for each jump height you want to include on a jump (more if you're making a double or triple bar jump).

Buy or Build?

Jump cups cost about $1 each to make or about $2-$3 each if you buy them. Commercial sources for jump cups are listed in the "Resource Guide" at beginning of the book.

Be aware that making your own jump cups is time-consuming; practically speaking, when you factor in labor, it's probably less expensive to buy jump cups. However, if you do want to make your own, plans are provided in this chapter.

Mounting the Cups

Follow the instructions below to mount the jump cups you have selected.

Materials Needed

- 1 – scrap piece of schedule 40 PVC that is the same diameter as the PVC you are using to make your jump bars
- 2 – jump cups for each jump height you want on any single-bar jump
- 1 – box #8 x 1" galvanized exterior drywall screws or whatever screws came with commercially-bought jump cups or were recommended by the manufacturer
- Duct tape or PVC cement

Tools Needed

- Scissors-type PVC cutting shears
- Drill with $^1/_8$" bit and Phillips head bit
- Carpenter's ruler or tape measure
- Pencil or marker

Directions

1. Set up the jump on a flat surface.

2. Determine what jump heights you want. Consult the rulebook for the appropriate agility organization(s) if you are not sure.

3. Measuring from the ground up, mark the jump heights you want on the vertical pieces of PVC where the jump cups will be attached (called the uprights).

4. Cut a 1"-2" long scrap piece of 1" PVC (or whatever diameter pipe you are using to make your jump bars), lay it in a spare jump cup, and either glue it or use duct tape to secure it in place.

5. Holding the scrap piece secured in the cup, align it so that the *top of the bar* in the cup is at one of the height marks you made on the upright. (All organizations measure jump heights to the top of the bar, not the middle or bottom, so the thickness of the bar is significant.) Make a mark on the upright where the *bottom* of the jump cup is located. Repeat for all the jump heights you originally marked.

6. Take a real jump cup, line up the bottom edge on each of your new marks, and make pencil marks through the holes drilled in the cups.

7. Drill $^1/_8$" pilot holes on your marks.

8. Drive screws through the holes in each cup into the upright using a drill with a Phillips head bit or a power screwdriver if you have one.

Jump Bars

Jump bars can be 48"-60" long. I recommend 48" jump bars if space is at a premium. I make all my jump bars the same length so that they are interchangeable between jumps. Nothing is more frustrating than searching for the "right" set of bars for a particular jump. If you inherit someone else's mess, you may want to use vinyl tape (required anyway) to color code the bars to the jumps so that you can keep things straight.

If the jumps are for competition, make at least two bars for each single jump, four bars for each double, and three bars for each triple. It's a good idea to make 10 or 12 extra bars so that you have them available if required at a trial.

1" schedule 40 PVC (which actually has an outside diameter of 1 ¼") is ideal for making jump bars since it complies with the rules of all the organizations, and it is what I recommend using unless the plans call for something different. Although 1 ¼" schedule 40 PVC also meets the specifications, the resulting bars will be heavy and unwieldy. Using ¾" schedule 40 PVC is acceptable under AKC and NADAC rules, but not under USDAA rules. See the table below for specifics.

NOTE: When you shop for PVC and use these plans, it's important to note that the width of pipe is always described by its *inside* diameter. However, agility regulations refer to the *outside* diameter measurement.

Organization	Min. Outside Diameter	Max. Outside Diameter
AKC	None specified	1 ³/₄"
NADAC/ASCA	³/₄"	None specified
USDAA	1 ¹/₄"	1 ³/₄"

For reasons of visibility, all jump bars must be marked with contrasting colors either by striping or banding them with tape.

Making the Bars

Materials Needed

- 1 – 10' length of schedule 40 PVC for each *pair* of jump bars you want to make

    NOTE: 1" PVC is recommended for jump bars unless the plans call for something different.

- 1 – roll colored tape

    NOTE: I prefer to use Color Code Self-Sticking Tape from Industrial Safety Company, part #2459 to #2468, depending on the color. Vinyl tape holds up better than cloth tape. Also be aware that all colors eventually fade with prolonged exposure to sunlight. However, blues and violets will fade the quickest.

Tools Needed

- Scissors-type PVC cutting shears
- Carpenter's ruler or tape measure
- Pencil or marker

Directions

1. From each 10' length of PVC pipe, cut two pieces that are the same length using the PVC shears.

2. Wrap colored tape around each bar in bands or in a spiral pattern.

Plans Included Here

In this chapter, you will find the following plans:

- Plastic Jump Cups
- Nonwinged Jump—Design #1
- Nonwinged Jump—Design #2
- Winged Jump with Plastic Lattice
- Panel Jump
- AKC Double Bar Jump
- USDAA Spread Jump
- Triple Bar Jump or Extended Spread Jump
- PVC Training Tire Jump
- Trombone Tire Jump
- Easily Adjustable Competition Tire
- Plastic Broad Jump with Built-In Marking Poles
- Wooden Broad Jump with Marking Poles

plastic jump cups

jump cups cost about $1 each to make or about $2-$3 each if you buy them. Commercial sources for jump cups are listed in the "Resource Guide" at the beginning of the book. You will need two jump cups for each jump height you want to include on a jump (more if you're making a double or triple bar jump).

Materials Needed

- 1 – 1" PVC male end plug (Spears part #D2466) for each jump cup you wish to make.

  NOTE: If you can't find these, you can use 1" PVC end caps instead. However, the end caps don't work quite as well as the male end plugs which have a thick, hexagonal base. If you do decide to use end caps, make sure the top is *flat,* not domed.

Tools Needed

- Hacksaw (preferred) or Dremel tool with heavy-duty cutting wheel
- Scissors-type PVC cutting shears (optional)
- Drill with $1/8$" bit and countersink bit
- Bench vise or vise grips
- Carpenter's ruler or tape measure
- Pencil or marker

Directions

The steps for making the jump cups are the same whether you are using PVC end caps or male PVC plugs.

1. Turn the plug on its side and clamp it into a bench vise with the cylindrical part sticking out. If you do not have a bench vise, you

will need an assistant who truly loves and trusts you to hold the plug with vise grips while you cut.

2. Make a vertical cut as shown in Figure 1. This cut is made parallel to, and as close as possible to, the inside edge of the plug but does *not* go all the way to the bottom—you need to leave between $1/8$" and $1/4$" of plastic at the bottom of the cut.

3. If you are using a hacksaw, make a horizontal cut that meets the bottom of your vertical cut as shown in Figure 1. If you are using a Dremel tool with a cutting wheel or PVC cutting shears, make two horizontal cuts as shown. Remove the excess piece you've cut away to reveal a near-perfect jump cup as shown in Figure 2.

4. Drill two holes through the flat back of the jump cup for mounting screws. Use the countersink bit to widen the top of each hole so that the screw heads will not protrude from the back of the cup when you mount it.

5. Repeat steps 1-4 until you have made as many jump cups as you need.

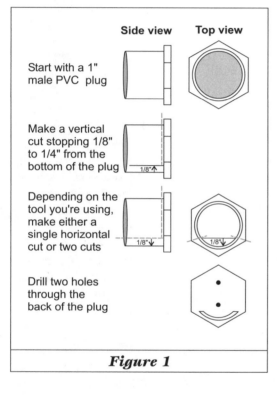

Start with a 1"
male PVC plug

Make a vertical
cut stopping 1/8"
to 1/4" from the
bottom of the plug

Depending on the
tool you're using,
make either a
single horizontal
cut or two cuts

Drill two holes
through the
back of the plug

Side view **Top view**

1/8"

1/8" 1/8"

Figure 1

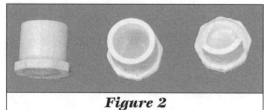

Figure 2

*N*onwinged jump—design #1

these plans are for a simple nonwinged jump that costs about $10 to make, not including jump cups.

Materials Needed

- 2 – 10' lengths $^3/_4$" schedule 40 PVC
- 4 – $^3/_4$" PVC tees
- 6 – $^3/_4$" PVC end caps
- PVC cement
- Jump cups and bars as described below

Jump Cups and Bars

- You will need two jump cups for each jump height. Purchase jump cups from one of the sources listed at the beginning of the book or make your own following the steps on page 23.
- You will also need to make two 48" jump bars (see page 22). Because of the design of this particular jump, the bars cannot be longer or shorter than 48".

Tools Needed

- Hacksaw, Dremel tool with heavy-duty cutting wheel, or PVC pipe cutter
- Carpenter's ruler or tape measure
- Pencil or marker

Directions

1. Cut the following pieces from the $^3/_4$" PVC:

   2 – 36" long
   6 – 18" long
   1 – 49" long

2. Glue together the PVC pipe and parts for each side of the jump (called a jump standard) as shown in Figure 1.

3. Connect the left and right jump standards by inserting the 49" piece of pipe into the open end of the tee on each one.

   NOTE: Do *not* glue the 49" piece in place. This piece of pipe rests on the ground and acts as a spacer to keep the jump standards at the right alignment so that bars will fit perfectly.

4. Attach jump cups to each jump standard. If you need help refer to the instructions for "Mounting the Cups" on page 21.

5. Place the jump on a flat surface and set your 48" long jump bars in the cups.

6. Make sure the bars are easily displaceable. If they are too tight, replace the 49" pipe between the jump standards with a longer piece of PVC. If the bars are too loose, cut a bit off the spacer piece and check the bars again.

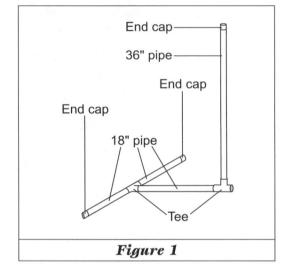

Figure 1

*N*onwinged jump—design #2

these plans are for another style of nonwinged jump. The design is essentially the same as in the previous set of plans, but this jump is easier to make thanks to furniture-grade PVC 4-way fittings. However, because of the special parts, this jump also costs slightly more to make (about $15, not including jump cups).

NOTE: This is a great jump to make from colored PVC. Just substitute 1 $^1/_4$" PVC pipe and fittings from one of the suppliers of colored PVC in the "Resource Guide" for the 1" pipe and parts called for in the materials list.

Materials Needed

- 2 – 10' lengths 1" schedule 40 PVC
- 2 – 1" PVC 4-way tee

  NOTE: The 4-way tees are a special part not found in home centers or plumbing supply stores. They must be ordered from one of the vendors listed in the "Resource Guide" at the beginning of this book under "Furniture-Grade PVC Pipe and Parts." When you're shopping, be aware that while this fitting is usually called a 4-way tee, several vendors refer to it as a 4-way ell or even a 4-way TL. Just make sure it looks like the fittings shown here!
- 6 – 1" PVC end caps
- PVC cement
- Jump cups and bars as described below

Jump Cups and Bars

- You will need two jump cups for each jump height. Purchase jump cups from one of the sources listed at the beginning of the book or make your own following the steps on page 23.
- You will also need to make two 48" jump bars (see page 22). Because of the design of this particular jump, the bars cannot be longer or shorter than 48".

Tools Needed

- Hacksaw, Dremel tool with heavy-duty cutting wheel, or PVC pipe cutter
- Carpenter's ruler or tape measure
- Pencil or marker

Directions

1. Cut the following pieces from the 1" PVC:

   2 – 36" long
   4 – 18" long
   1 – 49" long

2. Glue together the PVC pipe and parts for each side of the jump (called a jump standard) as shown in Figure 1.

3. Connect the left and right jump standards by inserting the 49" piece of pipe into the open end of the 4-way tee on each one.

   NOTE: Do *not* glue the 49" piece in place. This piece of pipe rests on the ground and acts as a spacer to keep the jump standards at the right alignment so that bars will fit perfectly.

4. Attach jump cups to each jump standard. If you need help refer to the instructions for "Mounting the Cups" on page 21.

5. Place the jump on a flat surface and set your 48" long jump bars in the cups.

6. Make sure the bars are easily displaceable. If they are too tight, replace the 49" pipe between the jump standards with a longer piece of PVC. If the bars are too loose, cut a bit off the spacer piece and check the bars again.

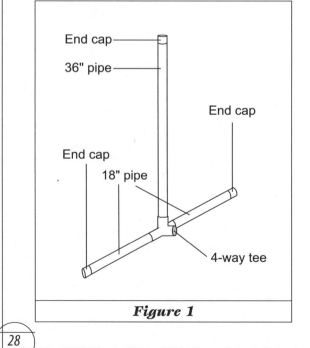

End cap

36" pipe

End cap

End cap

18" pipe

4-way tee

Figure 1

Winged jump with plastic lattice

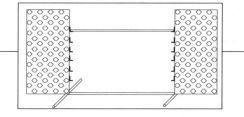

jump wings can be made with plywood inserts cut with a jigsaw or bandsaw and painted in all manner of interesting and attractive designs. However, you need to have an artistic bent for this, which I do not. These plans use plastic garden lattice to decorate the wings. If you prefer, you can leave out the lattice and use the PVC framework of the basic wings as a starting point for your own ideas.

Materials Needed

- 3 – 10' lengths $^3/_4$" schedule 40 PVC
- 6 – $^3/_4$" PVC 90° elbows
- 2 – $^3/_4$" PVC tees
- 2 – $^3/_4$" PVC 4-way crosses
- 4 – $^3/_4$" PVC end caps
- 1 – sheet 4' x 8' Tuff Bilt Lattice Classic Diamond Winter White

   NOTE: You may have to shop around for this. Check your local home center or call Plastics Research Corp. at (800) 394-6679 for a vendor. If you can't find it, or you want the wings to be a color other than white, any other wing covering (such as plywood) will do.

- 1 – box #8 x 1" galvanized exterior drywall screws
- PVC cement
- Jump cups and bars as described below

Jump Cups and Bars

- You will need two jump cups for each jump height. Purchase jump cups from one of the sources listed at the beginning of the book or make your own following the steps on page 23.

- You will also need to make two 48" jump bars (see page 22). Because of the design of this particular jump, the bars cannot be longer or shorter than 48".

Tools Needed

- Hacksaw, Dremel tool with heavy-duty cutting wheel, or PVC pipe cutter
- Circular saw
- Drill with $^1/_8$" bit and Phillips head bit
- Spring-loaded clamps
- Level
- Carpenter's ruler or tape measure
- Pencil or marker

Making the Wings

1. Cut the following pieces from the $^3/_4$" PVC:

   4 – 36" long
   6 – 18" long
   2 – 1 $^1/_2$" long
   1 – 49" long

   Put aside the remaining pipe as you'll need to cut two more pieces in step 4.

2. Glue together the pieces for each wing base as shown in Figure 1. Make sure that the open ends of the elbow and tee, which point up, align perfectly with each other. (It may help to insert scrap pieces of PVC into the holes to get everything lined up. Of course, don't acci-

dentally glue the scrap pieces!) Don't worry if there is some pipe showing between the cross and the tee.

3. Assemble the framework for each wing by gluing a 36" piece of PVC into the top hole of each elbow and the center hole of each tee. Use a level to make sure these pieces are straight up and down.

4. Select one of the wing assemblies. Place a 90° elbow on the end of each 36" vertical piece with the open mouths facing each other. Do *not* glue! Measure the distance between the two elbows as shown in Figure 2. Be sure to allow for the recess in each elbow joint where the pipe fits. Usually there is a slight seam on the outside of the elbow indicating where the "stop" is in the recess. Cut two pieces of $^3/_4$" PVC to the length you have measured, one for each wing assembly.

5. Test fit the pieces you cut into each wing assembly. The frame of each wing should now form a perfect rectangle. It is *very* important that the two vertical pieces of the wing frame are exactly parallel to each other or the bars will bind and not displace correctly. PVC is cheap; cut and recut if necessary to get this right. When you are satisfied that all is well, glue the elbows and the final horizontal piece in place for each wing.

6. Use the 49" piece of PVC pipe you cut to connect the two wings.

NOTE: Do *not* glue the 49" piece in place. This piece of pipe rests on the ground and acts as a spacer to keep the jump wing at the right alignment so that bars will fit perfectly.

7. Attach jump cups to the upright on each wing. If you need help refer to the instructions for "Mounting the Cups" on page 21.

8. Place the jump on a flat surface and set your 48" jump bars in the cups.

9. Make sure the bars are easily displaceable. If they are too tight, replace the 49" pipe between the jump wings with a longer piece of PVC. If the bars are too loose, cut a bit off the spacer piece and check the bars again.

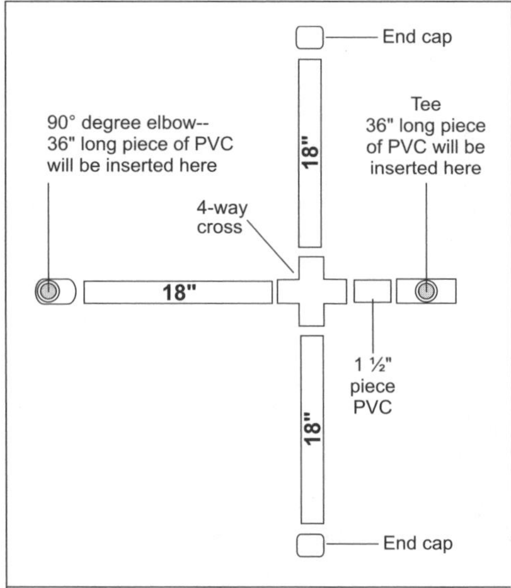

Finishing the Wings

1. Determine the width and height of each wing, measuring from the outside edges of the pipe and not including the joints.

2. Clamp the PVC lattice to a scrap piece of plywood or other board. Use a circular saw or Dremel tool to cut two pieces of PVC lattice to the exact size needed to cover the wing.

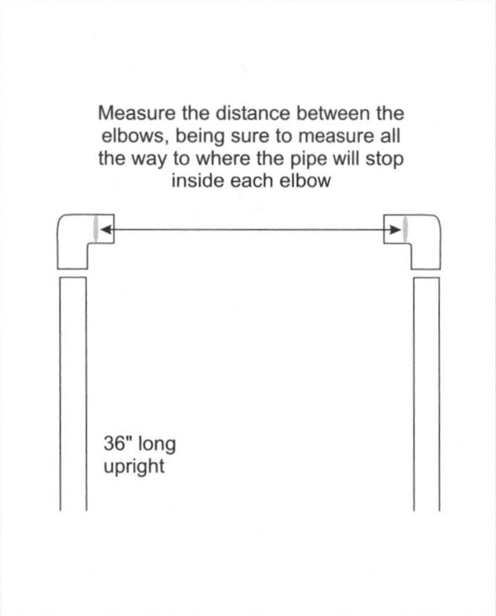

   NOTE: You will also need to cut out a small piece at the bottom of each lattice panel to make room for the stabilizing legs extending out of the PVC 4-way cross on the jump base.

3. Attach a lattice panel to each wing using the drywall screws.

Figure 1

End cap

Tee
36" long piece of PVC will be inserted here

90° degree elbow--
36" long piece of PVC will be inserted here

4-way cross

18"

18"

18"

1 ½" piece PVC

End cap

Figure 2

Measure the distance between the elbows, being sure to measure all the way to where the pipe will stop inside each elbow

36" long upright

panel jump

to make a panel jump, you need jump cups mounted to wings and a series of panels. Wooden panels are easy to make, but the wings for them need to be heavy to keep from tipping over. For backyard or light club use, you can make a panel jump from PVC. These plans are for building that kind of jump. Total cost is $60-$80, depending on how many jump heights you need and whether you make or purchase the jump cups.

Materials Needed

- 3 – 10' lengths $^3/_4$" schedule 40 PVC
- 3 – 10' lengths $^1/_2$" schedule 40 PVC
- 6 – $^3/_4$" PVC 90° elbows
- 2 – $^3/_4$" PVC tees
- 2 – $^3/_4$" PVC 4-way crosses
- 4 – $^3/_4$" PVC end caps
- 1 – sheet 4' x 8' Tuff Bilt Lattice Classic Diamond Winter White

  NOTE: You may have to shop around for this. Check your local home center or call Plastics Research Corp. at (800) 394-6679 for a vendor. If you can't find it, or you want the wings to be a color other than white, any other wing covering (such as plywood) will do.

- 2 – 8" wide x 12' long vinyl fascia boards (vinyl siding) shaped as shown in "Making the Panels"

  NOTE: Home center employees will swear they don't carry this, but they do! Keep asking until you get what you want.

- 15 – #6 or #8 x $^1/_2$" or $^5/_8$" flat-head Phillips screws
- 1 – box #8 x 1" galvanized exterior drywall screws
- PVC cement
- Jump cups as described in the next section

Jump Cups

- You will need two jump cups for each jump height. Purchase jump cups from one of the sources listed at the beginning of the book or make your own following the steps on page 23.

Tools Needed

- Hacksaw, Dremel tool with heavy-duty cutting wheel, or PVC pipe cutter
- Circular saw
- Drill with $^1/_8$" bit and Phillips head bit
- Spring-loaded clamps
- Level
- Carpenter's ruler or tape measure
- Pencil or marker

Making the Wings

1. Cut the following pieces from the $^3/_4$" PVC:

   4 – 36" long
   6 – 18" long
   2 – 1 $^1/_2$" long
   1 – 49" long

   Put aside the remaining PVC as you'll need to cut more in step 4.

2. Glue together the pieces for each wing base as shown in Figure 1. Make sure that the open ends of the elbow and tee, which point up, align perfectly with each other. (It may help to insert scrap pieces of PVC into the holes to get everything lined up. Of course, don't accidentally glue the scrap pieces!) Don't worry if there is some pipe showing between the cross and the tee.

3. Assemble the framework for each wing by gluing a 36" piece of PVC into the top hole of each elbow and the center hole of each tee. Use a level to make sure these pieces are straight up and down.

4. Select one of the wing assemblies. Place a 90° elbow on the end of each 36" vertical piece with the open mouths facing each other. Do *not* glue! Measure the distance between the two elbows as shown in Figure 2. Be sure to allow for the recess in each elbow joint where the pipe fits. Usually there is a slight seam on the outside of the elbow

indicating where the "stop" is in the recess. Cut two pieces of $^3/_4$" PVC to the length you have measured, one for each wing assembly.

5. Test fit the pieces you cut into each wing assembly. The frame of each wing should now form a perfect rectangle. It is *very* important that the two vertical pieces of the wing frame are exactly parallel to each other or the bars will bind and not displace correctly. PVC is cheap; cut and recut if necessary to get this right. When you are satisfied that all is well, glue the elbows and the final horizontal piece in place for each wing.

6. Use the 49" piece of PVC pipe you cut to connect the two wings.

NOTE: Do *not* glue the 49" piece in place. This piece of pipe rests on the ground and acts as a spacer to keep the jump wing at the right alignment so that bars will fit perfectly.

7. Measuring from the ground up, make marks on the upright of each wing at 4", 8", 12", 16", 20", and 24". Attach jump cups to each upright. For this jump, be sure to use a $^1/_2$" scrap piece of PVC pipe to align the jump cups. See "Mounting the Cups" on page 21.

Finishing the Wings

You can finish the wings by attaching painted plywood cutouts or using any one of a number of clever designs. Let your imagination be the guide. If you would like to use PVC lattice to finish your jump wings, follow these steps:

1. Determine the width and height of each wing, measuring from the outside edges of the pipe and not including the joints.

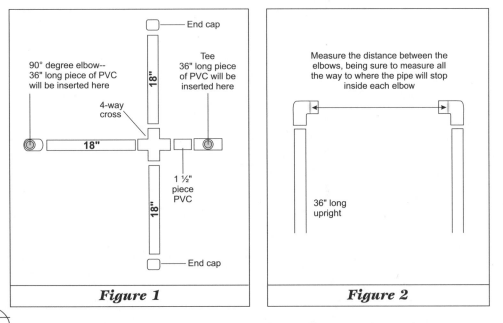

Figure 1

Figure 2

2. Clamp the PVC lattice to a scrap piece of plywood or other board. Use a circular saw or Dremel tool to cut two pieces of PVC lattice to the exact size needed to cover the wing.

    NOTE: You will also need to cut out a small piece at the bottom of each lattice panel to make room for the stabilizing legs extending out of the PVC 4-way cross on the jump base.

3. Attach a lattice panel to each wing using the drywall screws.

Making the Panels

Use the information in the table below to figure out how many panels you need to make for your jump.

AKC

Jump Height	Panels Needed & Order (Ground Up)
4"	one 3"
8"	one 3", one 4"
12"	one 3", two 4"
16"	one 3", three 4"
20"	one 3", four 4"
24"	one 3", five 4"

USDAA

Jump Height	Panels Needed & Order (Ground Up)
12"	one 5", one 6"
16"	one 5", one 6", one 4"
22"	one 5", one 6", one 4", one 6"
26"	one 5", one 6", one 4", one 6", one 4"

1. Cut the ¹/₂" PVC pipe into 48" long pieces. You will need a piece for each panel. So, if you want six panels for your jump, cut six 48" long pieces.

2. Cut the vinyl fascia to 47" lengths using a Dremel tool or circular saw. You will get three panels from each 12' long piece of siding.

3. Measure and cut each panel to the correct width (see the tables above). Note that the grooves in the siding are at 2" intervals. When cutting, it will help to clamp the board to a scrap piece of lumber, then mark, and cut through the vinyl fascia and lumber with a circular saw or Dremel tool.

4. Slip a piece of the ¹/₂" pipe you cut into the groove of each panel as shown in Figure 3. Check to see that it is centered side to side, then drill three pilot holes from the top of the panel into the pipe. Spread some PVC cement where the pieces are in contact and then rejoin the pipe and siding, lining up the pilot holes. Secure the assembly with the short flathead Phillips screws.

5. Set the panels in place and mark the sequence. The 5" (USDAA) or 3" (AKC) board is the bottom board. It's a good idea to label these boards with 2" or 3" tall press-on numbers, available at crafts or hardware stores. Alternatively, use a permanent marker.

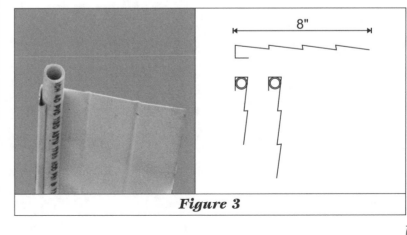

Figure 3

@KC double bar jump

for the regular AKC agility classes, the cups on the double bar jump are set at a width equal to half of the jump height (for example, 8" wide for the 16" jump height class). For the AKC Preferred class, you will also need a set of cups that are 4" high and 4" apart. (For instructions on measuring the width of a jump, refer to the beginning of this chapter.)

Materials Needed

- 6 – 10' lengths of 1" schedule 40 PVC
- 16 – 1" PVC 3-way ells

  NOTE: The 3-way ells are a special part not found in home centers or plumbing supply stores. They must be ordered from one of the vendors listed in the "Resource Guide" at the beginning of this book under "Furniture-Grade PVC Pipe and Parts."
- 1 – box #8 x 2" galvanized exterior drywall screws
- PVC cement
- Jump cups and bars as described below

Jump Cups and Bars

- You will need 24 jump cups. Purchase jump cups from one of the sources listed at the beginning of the book or make your own following the steps on page 23.
- You will also need at least four jump bars (see page 22).

Tools Needed

- Drill with ¹/₈" and ¹/₁₆" bits and Phillips driver bit
- Scissors-type PVC cutting shears
- Carpenter's ruler or tape measure
- Pencil or marker

Making the Wings

1. Using the PVC shears, cut the 1" PVC into the lengths specified below. To help you conserve PVC, I have specified what pieces to cut from each of the 10' lengths of pipe.

    - Pipe 1 and Pipe 2
      3 – 33" long
      1 – 21" long
    - Pipe 3
      2 – 33" long
      2 – 21" long
      1 – 12" long
    - Pipe 4
      4 – 21" long
      3 – 12" long
    - Pipe 5
      4 – 30" long
    - Pipe 6
      4 – 12" long

    When you're done cutting, check to be sure you have the following:

    - 8 – 33" pieces
    - 4 – 30" pieces
    - 8 – 21" pieces
    - 8 – 12" pieces

    You should have 72" of pipe left over to fix any mistakes. This is a good time to check that all of the pieces which are supposed to be the same length are within a hairsbreadth of each other (for example, all of the 33" pieces are the same length, the 30", and so on).

2. Collect two 33" pieces of PVC and two 21" pieces. Without gluing, assemble these into a rectangle using four 3-way ells, one at each corner as shown in Figure 1. Be sure that the open mouths of each of the 3-way ells faces in the same direction. Once you are sure that everything lines up and fits together correctly, take the assembly apart,

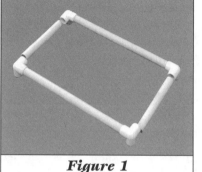

Figure 1

spread PVC cement on both parts of each joint (connector and pipe), and glue the rectangle together. Make three more of these rectangles.

3. Collect two of the rectangles you just made and four 12" pieces of PVC. Join the two rectangles by gluing a 12" piece of pipe into the open end of each 3-way ell. The result

will be a "box" that is approximately 14" x 24" x 36". This is one of the jump wings. Repeat this step to make the other jump wing.

4. Take one wing and turn it so that the 14" x 24" side is resting on a flat surface and the 14" x 36" side is facing you as in Figure 2. On the bottom pipe, mark a point that is half its actual length; for example, if it is 13 $^7/_8$" rather than 14", you are going to have to do some fancy math to figure out that half of that is 6 $^{15}/_{16}$". Now, measuring from the ground up, make a mark at 27 $^1/_2$" on each of the long (36") vertical pipes. Repeat for the other wing.

5. It helps to have an assistant for this step. Take one wing and one of the 30" pieces of PVC and line up the pipe so that it just touches the bottom mark on the wing. The other end of the pipe should be close to the 27 $^1/_2$" mark as illustrated in Figure 3. Since the pipe is round, you need to eyeball it by looking just past the curve of the pipe, straight at the bottom mark. Using the $^1/_{16}$" bit, drill a pilot hole through the 30" diagonal pipe and into the horizontal pipe. Mount the bottom end of the diagonal pipe with a 2" drywall screw. Repeat this step to attach a second 30" diagonal pipe to the bottom pipe of the wing.

6. Rotate the other end of the diagonal pipe (if necessary) so that it crosses the vertical pipe at the 27 $^1/_2$" mark. Drill a pilot hole through the diagonal pipe and into the vertical pipe. If you want to check your work, rotate the diagonal pipe out of the way slightly and see if you have hit the mark; you can always redrill if you missed it. When things are lined up, drive in a

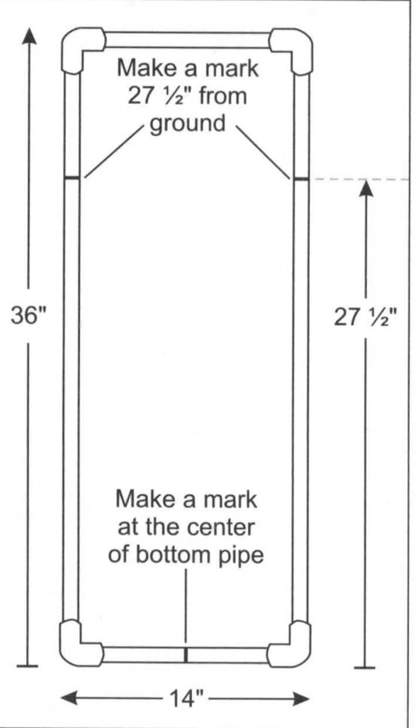

Figure 2

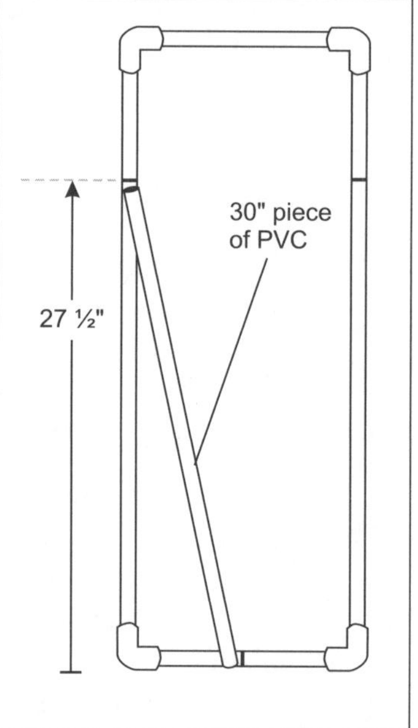

Make a mark 27 ½" from ground

36"

27 ½"

Make a mark at the center of bottom pipe

14"

Figure 3

27 ½"

30" piece of PVC

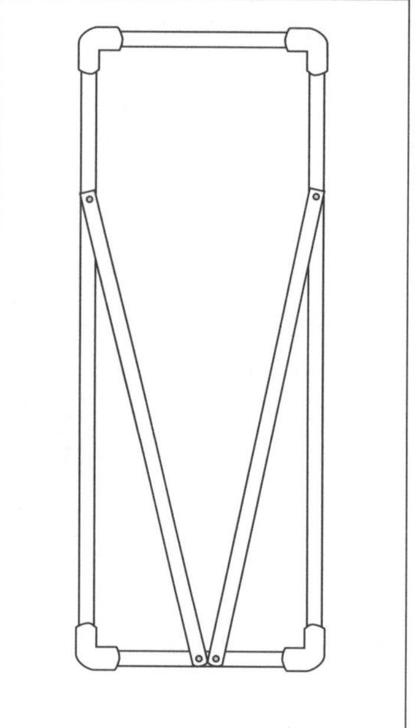

Figure 4

2" screw to hold the diagonal pipe at the top end. Repeat for the other diagonal pipe. You should end up with two pipes in a V-shape as shown in Figure 4.

7. Repeat steps 5 and 6 for the other jump wing. When you're done, push the two wings together so that the Vs line up. Make sure the Vs match on both sides. If they don't, the jump bars will set at funny angles.

Mounting the Jump Cups

1. On each diagonal pipe, make marks at 4", 8", 12", 16", 20", and 24". Measure from the ground up in a straight line. The marks should be 4", 4", 6", 8", 10", and 12" apart when measured from the center of the two diagonal pipes. That is, except for the bottom set, the marks should be half as far apart as the jump height. The bottom marks will be hard to get just right and you may have to fudge a bit. Under the rules, you are allowed $1/4$" deviation in height or a $1/2$" in width, so use that tolerance to your advantage for the lower bars.

   NOTE: If the measurements don't work out, you can move the diagonal pipes as needed to increase or decrease the jump span. Release the top of each V-shaped pair of bars by removing the screws. However, leave the screws nearest the point of the V in place. Rotate the bars until the measurements work out. Then drill new pilot holes and remount the top screws. Repeat this process for the other wing so that the wings match exactly. If you get the top set right—24" off the ground and 12" apart measured from the center of each bar—the others will fall into place automatically. That's trigonometry, which I told Mr. Spang I would never need to know.

2. Take a scrap piece of 1" PVC, lay it in a spare jump cup, and use duct tape or a rubber band to secure it in place. Align this "test bar" so that the *top of the bar* in the cup is at one of the height marks you made. Mark the location of the mounting hole for each jump cup. There will be six cups mounted on each diagonal pipe, at 4" height intervals, for a total of 24 cups.

3. Drill a pilot hole for each mark you made and then mount the cups using as many drywall screws as there are mounting holes in the jump cup.

4. Each finished wing should look like the one shown at the beginning of the plans. Double-check that all cups match by positioning the two wings with both sets of cups facing each other. The cups should be within a fraction of an inch of each other.

Decorating the Jump Wings

The 24" x 36" boxes forming your jump wings are a standard size that can be used to accommodate a variety of decorations. For example, I had a local sign shop make banners that size to attach to the wings. The banners had a grommet in each corner and I used a nylon cable tie to attach the corners to the PVC frame of each wing.

Another way to decorate the wings is to cut PVC lattice into 2' x 3' rectangles and mount these to the frame using #8 x 1" galvanized exterior drywall screws.

I have also used 36" PVC fencing which looks like a picket fence. It comes in 6' lengths so you can get three wing decorations out of each piece. The horizontal crosspieces of the fencing are hollow PVC. Use a small ($1/8$" bit) to drill a pilot hole all the way through this hollow rectangular bar and then a large ($1/2$") drill bit to drill through the same hole on *one side* only. This larger hole is used to feed a drywall screw into the inside of the rectangular bar so that the fence material can be mounted to the wing.

$\mathcal{U}$ SDAA spread jump

In USDAA Championship classes, a spread jump can be parallel for open dogs (dogs jumping 22" and 26"), meaning that both bars are set at the same height from the ground. The distance between the bars cannot be greater than 12"-15" on center. Parallel spreads are not allowed for mini dogs (dogs jumping 12" and 16"); rather, spreads for the mini dogs must always be ascending with the front bar set lower than the back bar. The distance of the spread is 10" to 12" on center and the front bar must be at least 4" lower than the back bar. Spread jumps are not used in the USDAA Performance classes. (For instructions on measuring the spread of a jump, refer to the beginning of this chapter.)

Materials Needed

- 6 – 10' lengths of 1" schedule 40 PVC
- 16 – 1" PVC 3-way ells

  NOTE: The 3-way ells are a special part not found in home centers or plumbing supply stores. They must be ordered from one of the vendors listed in the "Resource Guide" at the beginning of this book under "Furniture-Grade PVC Pipe and Parts."

- 1 – box #8 x 2" galvanized exterior drywall screws
- PVC cement
- Jump cups and bars as described below

Jump Cups and Bars

- You will need 16 jump cups. Purchase jump cups from one of the sources listed at the beginning of the book or make your own following the steps on page 23.
- You will also need at least four jump bars (see page 22).

Tools Needed

- Drill with $^1/_8$" and $^1/_{16}$" bits and Phillips driver bit
- Scissors-type PVC cutting shears

- Carpenter's ruler or tape measure
- Pencil or marker

Making the Jump Wings

1. Using the PVC shears, cut the 1" PVC into the lengths specified below. To help you conserve PVC, I have specified what pieces to cut from each of the 10' lengths of pipe.

- Pipe 1 and Pipe 2
  3 – 33" long
  1 – 21" long

- Pipe 3
  2 – 33" long
  2 – 21" long
  1 – 12" long

- Pipe 4
  4 – 21" long
  3 – 12" long

- Pipe 5
  4 – 30" long

- Pipe 6
  4 – 18" long
  4 – 12" long

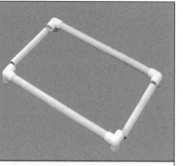

Figure 1

When you're done cutting, check to be sure you have the following:

- 8 – 33" pieces
- 4 – 30" pieces
- 8 – 21" pieces
- 4 – 18" pieces
- 8 – 12" pieces

This is a good time to check that all of the pieces which are supposed to be the same length are within a hairs-breadth of each other (for example, all of the 33" pieces are the same length, the 30", and so on).

2. Collect two 33" pieces of pipe and two 21" pieces. Without gluing, assemble these into a rectangle using four 3-way ells, one at each corner as shown in Figure 1. Be sure that the open mouths of each of the 3-way ells faces in the same direction. Once you are sure that everything lines up and fits together correctly, take the assembly apart, spread PVC cement on both parts of each joint (connector and pipe), and glue the rectangle together. Make three more of these rectangles.

3. Collect two of the rectangles you just made and four 12" pieces of PVC. Join the two rectangles by gluing a 12" piece of pipe into the open end of each 3-way ell. The result will be a "box" that is approximately 14" x 24" x 36". This is one of the jump wings. Repeat this step to make the other jump wing.

4. Take one wing and turn it so that the 14" x 24" side is resting on a flat surface and the 14" x 36" side is facing you as in Figure 2. On the bottom pipe, mark a point that is half its actual length; for example, if it is 13 $^{7}/_{8}$" rather than 14", you are going to have to do some fancy math to figure out that half of that is 6 $^{15}/_{16}$". Next, measuring from the ground up, make marks at 17 $^{1}/_{2}$" and 27 $^{1}/_{2}$" on each of the long (36") vertical pipes. Repeat for the other wing.

5. It helps to have an assistant for this step. Take one wing and one of the 30" pieces of PVC and line up the pipe so that it just touches the bottom mark on the wing. The other end of the pipe should be close to the 27 $^{1}/_{2}$" mark as shown in Figure 3. Since the pipe is round, you need to eyeball it by looking just past the curve of the pipe, straight at the center bottom mark. Using the $^{1}/_{16}$" bit, drill a pilot hole through the 30" diagonal pipe and into the horizontal pipe. Mount the bottom end of the diagonal pipe with a 2" drywall screw. Repeat this step to attach a second 30" diagonal pipe to the bottom pipe of the wing.

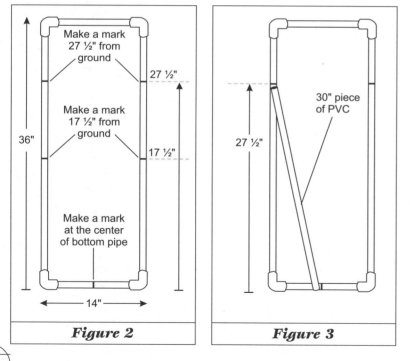

Figure 2

Make a mark 27 ½" from ground

27 ½"

Make a mark 17 ½" from ground

17 ½"

36"

Make a mark at the center of bottom pipe

14"

Figure 3

30" piece of PVC

27 ½"

6. Rotate the other end of the diagonal pipe (if necessary) so that it crosses the vertical pipe at the 27 ¹/₂" mark. Drill a pilot hole through the diagonal pipe and into the vertical pipe. If you want to check your work, rotate the diagonal pipe out of the way slightly and see if you have hit the mark; you can always redrill if you missed it. When things are lined up, drive in a 2" screw to hold the diagonal pipe at the top end. Repeat for the other diagonal pipe. You should end up with a V-shape as shown in Figure 4.

7. Add an 18" pipe on each side of the V you just formed as shown in Figure 5. The bottom ends of the 18" pipes should be pressed close against the bottom ends of the pipes forming the first V. The top ends of the 18" diagonal pipes will be close to the 17 ¹/₂" marks you made on the vertical pipes. (If you know triangles, it seems weird that the vertical measurement is so close to the length of the hypotenuse, or diagonal pipe. It seems weird to me, too. Some of the length is taken up by the thickness of the pipe and there is a small amount of clearance between the ground and the diagonal pipe which makes up some of the difference. Trust in the measurements, however.) Mount the bottom ends of the outer V by drilling pilot holes and attaching with drywall screws as you did for the first V.

8. Rotate the 18" pipes forming the outer V so that the ends of the pipe just cross the vertical bar of the wing. There will be about a 1" gap between the two arms of the V at the top end of the 18" pipes. Drill pilot holes and drive in drywall screws to fix the second V in place.

9. Finally, repeat steps 5 through 8 for the other jump wing. When you're done, push the two wings together so that the Vs line up. Make sure the Vs match on both sides. If they don't, the jump bars will set at funny angles.

Mounting the Jump Cups

1. Take one of the wings and on each of the diagonal pipes of the longer, inner V, make marks at 22" and 26". Measure from the ground up in a straight line. The marks should be 12" and 14 ¹/₂" apart when measured from the center of the two diagonal pipes; however, anything between 12" and 15" is acceptable.

2. On one of the shorter, outer V diagonal pipes—the one that will be at the front of your jump—make marks at 8" and 12" (still measuring from the ground up in a straight line). On the opposite short diagonal pipe, make marks at 12" and 16".

3. Repeat for the other wing, keeping in mind that because the bars will be ascending for the mini dogs, the wings must be *mirror images* of each other rather than identical clones. You must note the

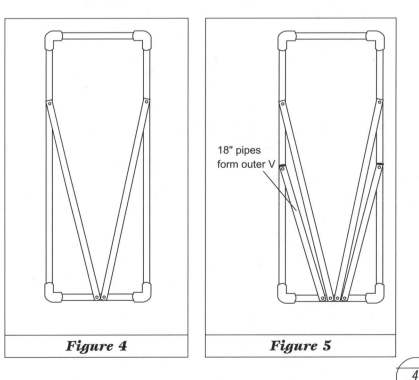

18" pipes form outer V

Figure 4   **Figure 5**

front and back of each wing so that the jump heights on the diagonal pipes of the shorter, outer V will be correct.

NOTE: If the measurements don't work out, you can move the diagonal pipes as needed to increase or decrease the jump span. Release the top of each V-shaped pair of bars by removing the screws. However, leave the screws nearest the point of each V in place. Rotate the bars until the measurements work out. Then drill new pilot holes and remount the top screws. Repeat this process for the other wing so that the wings match exactly.

4. Take a scrap piece of 1" PVC, lay it in a spare jump cup, and use duct tape or a rubber band to secure it in place. Align this "test bar" so that the *top of the bar* in the cup is at one of the height marks you made. Mark the location of the mounting hole for each jump cup. There will be four cups mounted on each diagonal pipe for a total of 16 cups.

5. Double-check that all cups match by positioning the two wings with both sets of cups facing each other. The cups should be within a fraction of an inch of each other.

Decorating the Jump Wings

The 24" x 36" boxes forming your jump wings are a standard size that can be used to accommodate a variety of decorations. For example, I had a local sign shop make banners that size to attach to the wings. The banners had a grommet in each corner and I used a nylon cable tie to attach the corners to the PVC frame of each wing.

Another way to decorate the wings is to cut PVC lattice into 2' x 3' rectangles and mount these to the frame using #8 x 1" galvanized exterior drywall screws.

I have also used 36" PVC fencing which looks like a picket fence. It comes in 6' lengths so you can get three wing decorations out of each piece. The horizontal crosspieces of the fencing are hollow PVC. Use a small ($1/8$" bit) to drill a pilot hole all the way through this hollow rectangular bar and then a large ($1/2$") drill bit to drill through the same hole on *one side* only. This larger hole is used to feed a drywall screw into the inside of the rectangular bar so that the fence material can be mounted to the wing.

*t*riple bar jump or extended spread jump

these plans are for making an AKC triple jump or a USDAA extended spread jump. (Triples are not used in NADAC.) Under USDAA rules, an *extended spread jump* is a spread jump set so that the front and back poles are 12" apart on center for mini dogs and 20" to 24" apart on center for big dogs. An extended spread can be made up of two or three like-kind hurdles placed closely together or it can be a single obstacle that simulates a double jump or a triple jump as in these plans. There is really no way to make a spread jump that is legal for both AKC and USDAA competition, so you will have to choose.

These plans are organized in two parts:

- Making the wings for the jump—these steps are the same whether you are building an AKC triple bar jump or a USDAA extended spread jump.
- Making a panel or slats to hold the jump cups needed—follow the set of steps labeled AKC or USDAA, depending on which jump you are building.

Making the Jump Wings

Follow the steps in this section whether you are making an AKC triple jump or a USDAA extended spread.

Materials Needed

- 5 – 10' lengths 1" schedule 40 PVC
- 6 – 1" PVC 90° elbows,
- 4 – 1" PVC 45° elbows
- 6 – 1" PVC tees
- 6 – 1" PVC 3-way ells

  NOTE: The 3-way ells are a special part not found in home centers or plumbing supply stores. They must be ordered from one of the vendors listed in the "Resource Guide" at the beginning of this book under "Furniture-Grade PVC Pipe and Parts."

- 1 – sheet 4' x 8' Tuff Bilt Lattice Classic Diamond Winter White

  NOTE: You may have to shop around for this. Check your local home center or call Plastics Research Corp. at (800) 394-6679 for a vendor. If you can't find it, or you want the wings to be a color other than white, any other wing covering (such as fabric or plywood) will do.

- 1 – box 1 ½" or 1 ⅝" exterior, fine-thread drywall screws
- PVC cement

Tools Needed

- Scissors-type PVC cutting shears or hacksaw
- Carpenter's ruler or tape measure
- Pencil or marker

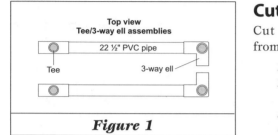

Top view
Tee/3-way ell assemblies

22 ½" PVC pipe

Tee

3-way ell

Figure 1

Cutting the PVC

Cut the following pieces from the 1" PVC:

2 – 33" long
2 – 32" long
10 – 22 ½" long
8 – 16" long
6 – 1 ½" long

Making the Wing Bases

Work on a flat surface and "test assemble" each part of the base *before* you glue to ensure that the joints are at right angles to each other.

1. Make two assemblies that are mirror images of each other—one for the left jump wing and one for the right—by putting a tee on one end of a 22 ½" length of PVC and a 3-way ell on the other as shown in Figure 1. The top "mouth" of each 3-way ell points upward. These will be referred to as the tee/3-way ell assemblies in subsequent steps.

2. Make the four corner assemblies shown in Figure 2. Two corners are assembled from 3-way ell, a 1 ½" piece of pipe, and a 45° elbow (corner assembly #1). The other two corners are assembled from a 90° elbow, a 45° elbow, and two 1 ½" pieces of PVC that are used as joiners (corner assembly #2).

3. Fit a 22 ½" piece of PVC into the open end of the 3-way ell on each assembly from step 1 (tee/3-way ell assemblies). You now have two L-shaped assemblies that are mirror images as shown in Figure 3.

4. Add a corner assembly #1 and #2 to each L-shaped assembly as shown in Figure 4. Then hold up a 32" piece of PVC next to the open ends of the 45° elbows as shown. If necessary, trim the length of pipe so that it will fit. Repeat for the other 32" piece of PVC. Take one of these pipes, gently push apart the two corner assemblies, spread glue on both joints, and ease the pipe into place to complete the frame. Repeat for the other wing base.

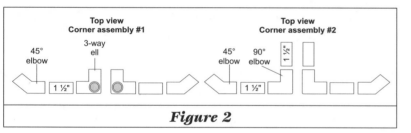

Top view
Corner assembly #1

45°
elbow

3-way
ell

1 ½"

Top view
Corner assembly #2

45°
elbow

90°
elbow

1 ½"

1 ½"

Figure 2

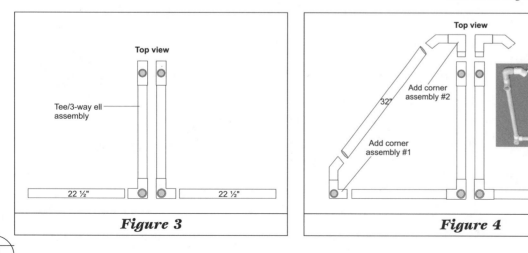

Top view

Tee/3-way ell
assembly

22 ½"

22 ½"

Figure 3

Top view

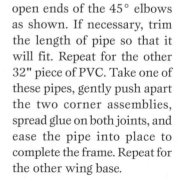

Add corner
assembly #2

32"

Add corner
assembly #1

Figure 4

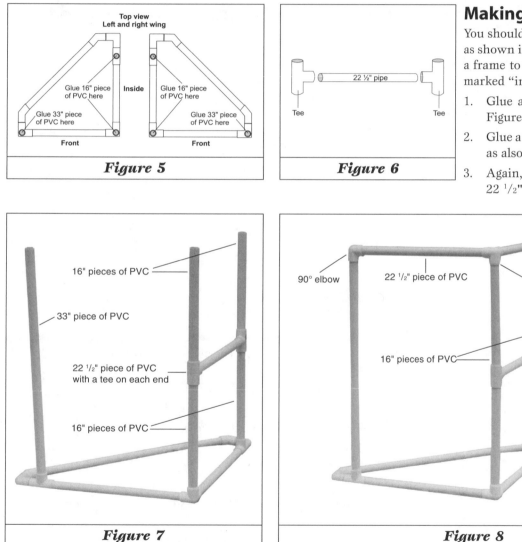

Top view
Left and right wing

Glue 16" piece of PVC here

Inside

Glue 16" piece of PVC here

Glue 33" piece of PVC here

Glue 33" piece of PVC here

Front

Front

Figure 5

22 ½" pipe

Tee

Tee

Figure 6

16" pieces of PVC

33" piece of PVC

22 ½" piece of PVC with a tee on each end

16" pieces of PVC

Figure 7

90° elbow

90° elbow

22 ½" piece of PVC

22 ½" piece of PVC

3-way ell

16" pieces of PVC

Figure 8

Making the Wing Frames

You should now have two triangular wing bases, left and right, as shown in Figure 5. For the area marked "front," you'll build a frame to hold the decorative front of the wing. For the area marked "inside," you'll build a frame to hold jump cups.

1. Glue a 33" long piece of PVC in each corner marked in Figure 5.

2. Glue a 16" long piece of PVC in each of the remaining holes as also shown in Figure 5.

3. Again, working on a flat surface, glue a tee on each end of a 22 ½" piece of PVC as shown in Figure 6. Then glue this assembly onto the two upright 16" pieces of PVC you glued in the previous step as shown in Figure 7.

4. Glue two more 16" pipes into each of the two open holes in the tees so that the two pipes stick up vertically as shown in Figure 8.

5. Finish the inside support assembly with a 3-way ell, a 22 ½" piece of PVC, and a 90° elbow as illustrated in Figure 8.

6. Use a 90° elbow and one last 22 ¹/₂" piece of PVC to connect the top 3-way ell to the vertical 33" piece at the back corner of the base. Glue these pieces in place.

7. Repeat steps 3-6 to build an identical front frame for the other jump wing base.

8. Complete the wings by attaching PVC lattice, fabric banners, or plywood cutouts to the front frames as shown in Figure 9. Use 1 ¹/₂" or 1 ⁵/₈" exterior, fine-thread drywall screws for this job.

NOTE: The lattice or decorative part of the wings is what will be *facing* the dog as it approaches the jump.

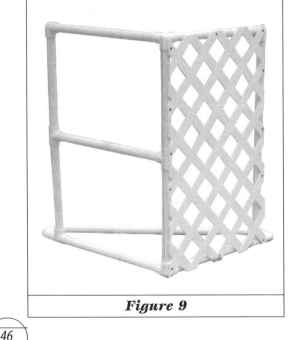

Figure 9

AKC Triple: Making Slats to Hold the Jump Cups

The triple bar jump has a series of three ascending bars. The horizontal distance between adjacent bars is equal to half of the jump height, while the vertical distance is one-quarter the jump height.

Height Division	Bar Heights	Distance Bet. Adjacent Bars
8"	4", 6", 8"	4"
12"	6", 9", 12"	6"
16"	8", 12", 16"	8"
20"	10", 15", 20"	10"
24"	12", 18", 24"	12"

NOTE: For the 4" jump height in the AKC Preferred class, only two bars are typically used: the first bar is set on the ground approximately 4" in front of the back bar, which is set at 4".

Materials Needed

- 3 – 8' lengths Tuff-Bilt Lattice Winter White "H" molding

  NOTE: This is used to hold together sheets of PVC lattice so you should be able to find this at the same store where you got the lattice. If not, substitute three 1" x 2" x 8' white wood furring strips.

- 2 – 10' lengths 1" schedule 40 PVC

- 1 – box 1 ¹/₂" or 1 ⁵/₈" exterior, fine-thread drywall screws

- Jump cups and bars as described below

Jump Cups and Bars

- You will need 30 jump cups. Purchase jump cups from one of the sources listed at the beginning of the book or make your own following the steps on page 23.

- You will also need at least three jump bars (see page 22).

Tools Needed

- Drill with $1/8$" and $5/32$" bits and Phillips head bit
- Dremel tool, hacksaw, or jigsaw or circular saw if using wood strips
- Carpenter's ruler or tape measure
- Pencil or marker

Directions

1. Cut the following pieces from the "H" molding:

   2 – 36" long (vertical strips)
   2 – 60" long (middle strips)
   2 – 27" long (third and lowest strips)

2. I mount the 36" strip first. Place the strip on the inside frame as shown in Figure 10. If it doesn't fit exactly, mark where it needs to be trimmed and cut it. Secure the strip in place with drywall screws.

3. The second, and longest, strip (60" length) is mounted from the bottom inside back corner to the top inside front corner as shown in Figure 10. Hold the strip in place and mark where you need to cut so that things fit neatly in the corners. You'll want to make an angled cut as shown. Double-check this measurement and your marks, cut the piece to fit, and mount it to the frame with drywall screws.

4. The 27" strip goes in the lowest position. Measure 12" up from a level surface to position the *center* of the bottom strip. It has the trickiest angle and should be cut by hand after marking.

5. The strips should make a 90°, 60°, and 30° angle with respect to a ground line. Using a Dremel tool, clean off any protruding edges.

6. Repeat steps 2 through 5 for the other wing.

7. Mount 15 jump cups on each wing in the positions indicated in Figure 11. Drill pilot holes into the molding or furring strips and use drywall screws to mount each jump cup.

   NOTE: For help measuring jump width or heights, refer to the beginning of this chapter.

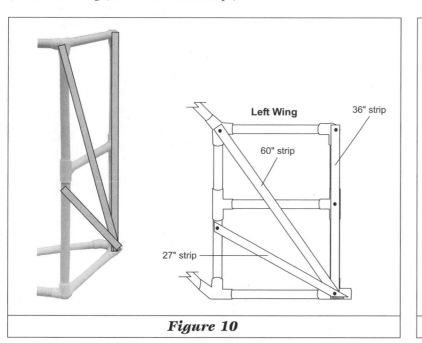

Left Wing
36" strip
60" strip
27" strip

Figure 10

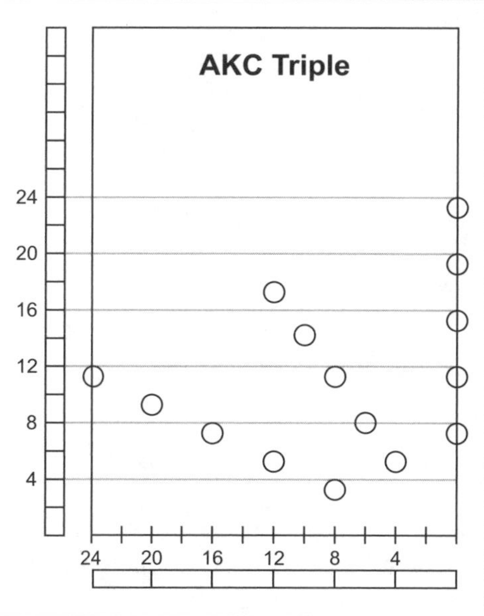

AKC Triple

Figure 11

USDAA Extended Spread: Making a Panel to Hold the Jump Cups

This jump has a series of three ascending bars. The bars will be set at the heights and spans listed below for each jump height division.

Height Division	Bar Heights	Distance Bet. Adjacent Bars
12"	6", 9", 12"	6"
18"	10", 13", 16"	6"
22"	16", 19", 22"	12"
26"	20", 23", 26"	12"

Materials Needed

- 1 – 3' x 6' clear acrylic sheet

  NOTE: This item should be available from your local home store. If not, you can order part #44336 from U.S. Plastics. The acrylic sheet is fragile and difficult to work with. You may prefer to use $1/4$" plywood or composite board instead. If you do, be sure to paint it before assembly.

- 24 – 6-32 x $3/4$" machine screws
- 24 – 6-32 machine nuts
- 36 – nylon washers for screws
- 12 – 1 $1/2$" or 1 $5/8$" exterior, fine-thread drywall screws
- Jump cups and bars as described below

Jump Cups and Bars

- You will need 24 jump cups. Purchase jump cups from one of the sources listed at the beginning of the book or make your own following the steps on page 23.
- You will also need at least three jump bars (see page 22).

Tools Needed

- Drill with $1/8$" and $5/32$" bits and Phillips bit
- Ratchet wrench with nut driver
- Carpenter's ruler or tape measure
- Pencil or marker

Directions

1. Cut the acrylic sheet so that you have two 24" x 36" panels.

2. Clamp a cut panel to the frame of each wing as shown in Figure 12. Drill six $1/8$" holes through each panel and into the PVC fittings (a hole in each corner and one in each middle fitting of the frame). Place a nylon washer on each drywall screw and insert the screws into the holes you drilled. Tighten them by hand if you are mounting an acrylic panel.

   NOTE: If you are using acrylic, be careful as the edges are sharp (you can sand them). The plastic is also brittle and easy to crack, so work slowly and carefully.

3. Mount 12 jump cups on each wing in the positions indicated in Figure 13. Drill $5/32$" holes through the panel for each jump cup and attach the cups using 6-32 x $3/4$" machine screws, a nylon washer to avoid cracking the panel, and a nut.

   NOTE: For instructions on measuring the width or spread of a jump as well as jump heights, please refer to the beginning of this chapter.

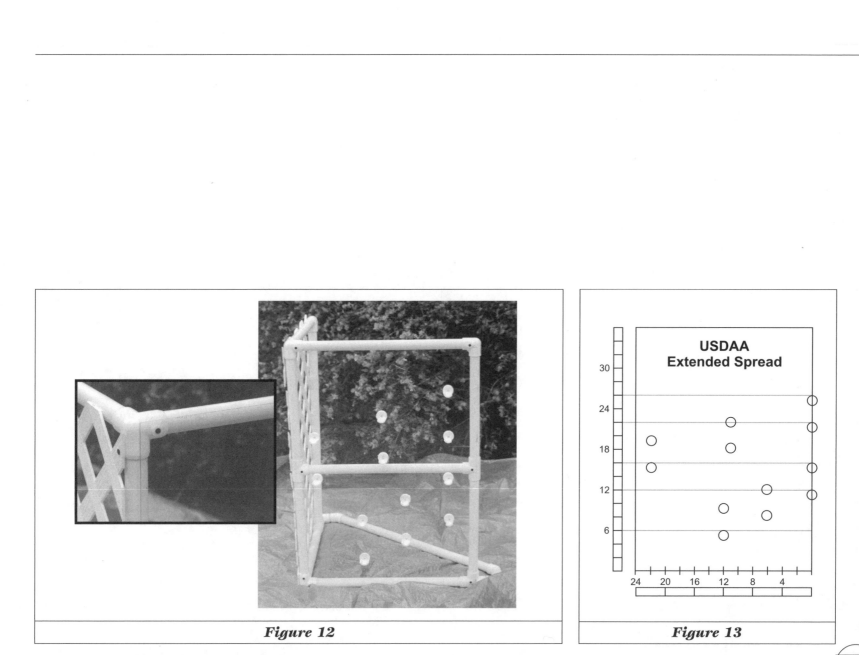

Figure 12

Figure 13

USDAA
Extended Spread

*p*VC training tire jump

although this tire jump is legal for competition, it is designed more for the backyard trainer or classroom. It is light and inexpensive, but requires more time for height changes. The estimated cost is $60.

Materials Needed

- 3 – 10' lengths 1 ¹/₄" schedule 40 PVC
- 2 – 1 ¹/₄" PVC 90° elbows
- 2 – 1 ¹/₄" PVC 4-way tees

  NOTE: The 4-way tees are a special part not found in home centers or plumbing supply stores. They must be ordered from one of the vendors listed in the "Resource Guide" at the beginning of this book under "Furniture-Grade PVC Pipe and Parts."

- 2 – ¹/₄" x 4" eyebolts (*not* eye screws)
- 6 – ¹/₄" x 3" eyebolts
- 1 – 10' length 4" drain pipe, black plastic (with or without drain slits)
- 1 – internal connector for drain pipe

  NOTE: Some people are reporting that these are difficult to find. The external connectors make a large ridge in the tire which I find ugly, but you can use them in a pinch.

- 4 – ¹/₄" fender washers
- 4 – ¹/₄" toggle bolts
- 1 – 10' length yellow plastic chain (used for decorative borders)
- 2 – 16" long bungee cords (measure the unstretched bungee; don't rely on the label)
- 2 – 2" breakable chain links, also called repair links

- 2 – ³/₈" snap bolts

  NOTE: The snap bolts can be the type with one end permanently mounted or the type with two snap ends.

- 2 – red electrical connectors or wire nuts

  NOTE: I use Scotchlok Twist Connect type R.

- 1 – roll silver duct tape
- 1 – roll colored plastic tape
- 3 – spray cans of expanding foam insulation (optional)
- PVC cement

Tools Needed

- PVC cutter, hacksaw, or Dremel tool with cutting wheel
- Drill with ¹/₄" and ³/₄" bits
- Carpenter's ruler or tape measure
- Pencil or marker

Cutting the PVC

Cut the following pieces from the 1 ¹/₄" PVC:

    2 – 60" long
    2 – 42" long (USDAA) *OR* 48" long (AKC)
    4 – 18" long

Assembling the Tire Frame

1. Assemble the vertical sides of the tire frame first. For each 60" long piece of PVC, glue a 4-way tee on one end and a 90° elbow on the other end. If you glue the 4-way tee on before the elbow, it's easier. Before the glue dries, lay the pipe down on a flat surface so that the horizontal "mouth" of the 4-way tee (see Figure 1) is exactly parallel to the horizontal mouth of the elbow.

   NOTE: Insert pieces of scrap PVC in the horizontal holes to help you get things lined up, but be sure not to glue them in.

2. Join the vertical sides with the two 42" or 48" pieces of PVC and glue.

3. Glue the four 18" legs in the remaining holes of the 4-way tees.

Attaching Mounting Hardware for the Tire

1. Once the PVC cement is dry, drill a ¹/₄" hole diagonally from the outside corner of each 90° elbow as close as possible to the inside corner (see "Outside Corner" enlargement in Figure 2). Don't worry if you miss by a

little bit. Place the 4" eyebolts through the hole you just made so that the eye is inside the tire frame. Use one of the nuts supplied with the bolts to secure the bolt. Then put a wire nut on the end of the bolt so that it doesn't protrude and cause a safety hazard.

2. Drill a hole just above each 4-way tee (see Figure 3). Make these holes parallel to the ground. Take a nut off one of the unused eyebolts

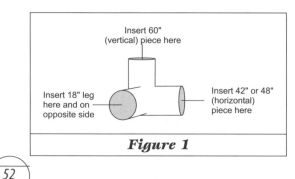

Figure 1

Insert 60" (vertical) piece here

Insert 18" leg here and on opposite side

Insert 42" or 48" (horizontal) piece here

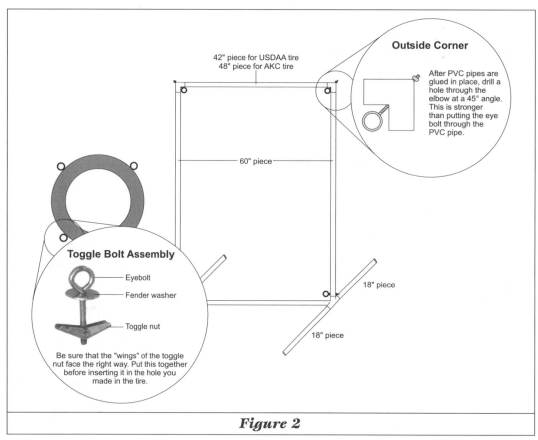

42" piece for USDAA tire
48" piece for AKC tire

Outside Corner

After PVC pipes are glued in place, drill a hole through the elbow at a 45° angle. This is stronger than putting the eye bolt through the PVC pipe.

60" piece

18" piece

18" piece

Toggle Bolt Assembly

Eyebolt

Fender washer

Toggle nut

Be sure that the "wings" of the toggle nut face the right way. Put this together before inserting it in the hole you made in the tire.

Figure 2

(you won't need it) and screw it on so that it's as close as possible to the eye. Insert this assembly through the hole you just made so that the eye and nut are inside the tire frame. Use another nut to secure the bolt in place—it will barely be long enough to reach.

Making the Tire

1. Cut the drain pipe to the length that you want. For a medium-sized USDAA tire (19" inner diameter), cut the drain pipe to 82". For an AKC tire (24" diameter), cut the pipe to 92". To figure your own tire size, take the diameter you want, add 7" for the width of the sidewall, and multiply by pi (3.14). This length will only be an estimate, since the pipe "scrunches" and changes its length.

2. Put the connector in one end of the cut drain pipe. Rip off four small pieces of duct tape. Divide the length of the drain pipe by 4. Measure this distance, starting 3" from the end of the pipe with the connector. Use a piece of tape to mark each position. For example, for an 82" piece of pipe, dividing by 4 gives you 20 $^1/_2$". You would mark the pipe in increments of 20 $^1/_2$", starting at 3". So you would put tape at 3", 23 $^1/_2$", 44", and 64 $^1/_2$".

3. Assemble the tire. *Warning! Once you click the connector into place, there is no turning back.* Bend the pipe around until it meets the connector, take a deep breath, and click it into place. It will be lopsided, but don't despair! Roll the "proto-tire" around on a hard, flat surface and push where it's too long. Rotate and push again. Continue rolling and pushing until you have a nice, round tire.

4. Mount the remaining four eyebolts onto the tire. Drill $^3/_4$" holes in the sides of the drain pipe where you made the four marks. One of the holes should go through the connector; this helps hold everything together. A piece of plastic from each drill hole will fall down inside the tire. Shake them out now through the drill holes or they will rattle around and drive you nuts later!

5. Remove the threaded bolts from the toggle bolts you purchased and discard them. You only need the spring-loaded toggle "nut." Slip a fender washer on an eyebolt and screw on a toggle nut so that it folds up toward the eye (see the "Toggle Bolt Assembly" inset in Figure 2). Turn the toggle nut so that it catches on the threads, but leave space between the toggle arms and the washer. Push the assembly into the $^3/_4$" hole and turn the eyebolt clockwise until it tightens inside the tire. Repeat for the rest of the eyebolts.

Figure 3

6. (Optional) To help keep the shape of the tire, you can fill it with expanding foam insulation. Using the $^3/_4$" bit, drill an extra four holes in the side of the tire. Lay the tire on a flat surface, open a can of expanding foam insulation, screw on the nozzle pipe, and let 'er rip into each of the four holes. Be sure to point the nozzle in both directions through each hole. Note that the foam continues to expand during the first few minutes. It takes about 2 ¼ cans to fill an AKC tire; a little less to fill a USDAA tire. Let the foam set overnight before proceeding. If any leaks out, cut away the excess with a utility knife.

7. Wrap the tire with duct tape. Start about midway between two eye-bolts with the tape at a slight angle so that you're wrapping in a continuous spiral. When you get to an eyebolt, try to make the middle of the tape end up straddling the bolt. Turn it parallel to the length of the tape, cut a small slit in the tape so that it slips over the eye, and then rotate the eye back into place. After you've put on a roll of duct tape, wrap the tire with the colored tape. Be sure to make some contrasting stripes so that the dog can easily see the tire. You can use a contrasting color or put another band of silver duct tape on top of the plastic.

NOTE: Wrapping uses a lot of duct tape, which is expensive. However, I've found that buying cheap tape is false economy; only major brands last outside for any length of time. I use a base layer of silver cloth duct tape (I prefer 3M) and then overlay that with colored plastic tape from Industrial Safety, which holds up better than cloth duct tape. Even so, your tire will need rewrapping every year or so.

Mounting the Tire

1. Cut two 36" lengths of plastic chain. Connect each chain to an upper, frame-mounted eyebolt using a snap bolt. Connect the other end to one of the eyebolts on the tire using a repair link.

2. Check the height of the tire by measuring from the bottom inside edge of the tire to the ground. Adjust the tire to one of the jump heights you will use and mark the appropriate chain links with pieces of colored tape, nail polish, or paint. Repeat the process and mark the other links that you will use most.

3. Hook a bungee cord between each of the bottom tire eyebolts and its corresponding eyebolt on the frame.

Figure 4

trombone tire jump

this type of tire jump is not legal for competition since the "trombone" is part of the frame. However, it adjusts easily from one height to another with only one hand, making it useful for classes where rapid height changes between dogs are needed. The estimated cost is $40 ($60 if you use furniture-grade PVC). Whatever type of PVC you buy, be sure that the 1" pipe fits inside the 1 ¼" pipe and slides smoothly.

Materials Needed

- 4 – 10' length 1" schedule 40 PVC pipe
- 1 – 10' length 1 ¼" schedule 40 PVC pipe
- 4 – 1" PVC tees
- 2 – 1" PVC 90° elbows
- 2 – 1" PVC 4-way tees

   NOTE: The 4-way tees are a special part not found in home centers or plumbing supply stores. They must be ordered from one of the vendors listed in the "Resource Guide" at the beginning of this book under "Furniture-Grade PVC Pipe and Parts."

- 2 – ¼" x 3" eyebolts (*not* eye screws)
- 1 – ¼" hex nut
- 1 – ¼" toggle bolt
- 1 – ¼" fender washer for eyebolt
- 1 – 10' length plastic chain (used for decorative borders)
- 1 – 10' length 4" drainpipe, black plastic (with or without drain slits)
- 1 – internal connector for drainpipe
- 1 – ⅜" snap hook (either the type with an end that can be mounted and a snap at the other end, or the type with a snap at each end)
- 2 – 2" breakable chain links (also called repair links)

- PVC cement
- 1 – roll silver duct tape
- 1 – roll colored plastic tape

Tools Needed

- PVC cutter, hacksaw, or Dremel tool with cutting wheel
- Drill with ¼" and ¾" bits
- Hole saw, 1 ⅝" diameter
- Level
- Carpenter's ruler or tape measure
- Pencil or marker

Making the Tire

1. Cut the drainpipe to the length you want. For a medium-sized USDAA tire (19" inner diameter), cut the drain pipe to 82". For an AKC tire (24" diameter), cut the pipe to 92". To figure your own tire size, take the diameter you want, add 7" for the width of the sidewall, and multiply by pi (3.14).

2. Assemble the tire. *Warning! Once you click the connector into place, there is no turning back.* Bend the pipe around until it meets the connector, take a deep breath, and click the loose end into place. It will be

Toggle Bolt Assembly

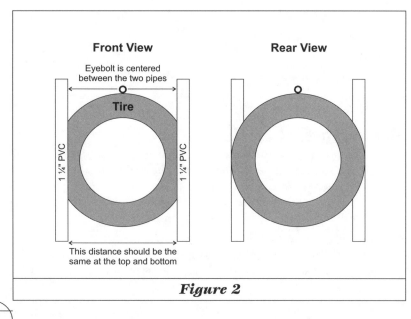

Eyebolt

Fender washer

Toggle nut

Be sure that the "wings" of the toggle nut face the right way.

Figure 1

all lopsided, but don't despair! Roll the "proto-tire" around on a hard, flat surface and push where it's too long. Rotate and push again. Continue rolling and pushing until you have a nice, round tire.

3. Drill a single $3/4$" hole in the tire near the joint with the connector. A piece of plastic from the drill hole will fall down inside the tire. Shake it out now or it will rattle around and drive you nuts later!

4. Remove the threaded bolt from the toggle bolt you purchased and discard it. You only need the spring-loaded toggle "nut." Slip a fender washer on an eyebolt and then screw

on a toggle nut so that it folds up toward the eye (see Figure 1). Turn the toggle nut so that it catches on the threads, but leave space between the arms of the toggle and the washer. Push the assembly into the $3/4$" hole and turn the eyebolt clockwise until it tightens inside the tire.

Cutting the PVC

1. Cut the following pieces from the 1" PVC:

   4 – 60" long

   8 – 18" long

   NOTE: Don't put away the 1" pipe as you'll need to cut two more pieces when you determine the correct length in step 4 of "Assembling the Frame."

2. Lay the tire on a flat surface and measure the *outside* diameter of the tire. Add 2" to this number and then cut two pieces of 1 $1/4$" PVC pipe to that length. These pieces will be between 27" and 33" depending on the size of the tire you made. For example, if you made a USDAA tire with an 18" inside di-

Front View

Eyebolt is centered between the two pipes

Tire

1 ¼" PVC

1 ¼" PVC

This distance should be the same at the top and bottom

Rear View

Figure 2

Top View

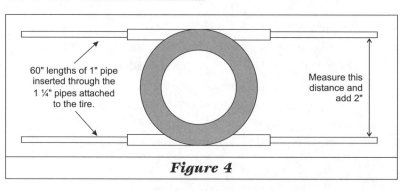

Tire

Pieces of 1 ¼" PVC pipe

Figure 3

60" lengths of 1" pipe inserted through the 1 ¼" pipes attached to the tire.

Measure this distance and add 2"

Figure 4

ameter, you need two 27" long pieces of pipe as the outside diameter will measure 25". If you made an AKC tire with a 24" inside diameter, the outside diameter will measure 31" so that you will need two 33" long pieces of 1 ¼" pipe.

Assembling the Frame

1. Take the two pieces you cut from the 1 ¼" PVC pipe and lay them on *top* of the tire so that the eyebolt is exactly halfway in between them, and the two pipes are parallel and aligned with the edges of the tire as shown in Figure 2. Measure the distance between the pipes at several points to make sure it is equal. You are going to cut four holes in the tire so that you can insert the pipes through the inside of the tire at their current positions. Mark the four places on the tire where the pipe should come through. Using the hole saw, cut a hole through the tire at each mark.

2. Slide a piece of 1 ¼" PVC through the holes you have made on each side of the tire as shown in Figure 3. Make sure the ends are even and the pipes are parallel before proceeding to the next step.

3. Begin wrapping the tire with duct tape. You want to wrap the tape around the tire and the PVC pipes so that they are tightly bound together to form a single unit. Wrap tape around the tire until it is completely bound with duct tape, then add contrasting stripes using a different color plastic tape.

4. Slide a 60" long piece of 1" PVC pipe inside each of the 1 ¼" pipes attached to the tire. Measure the distance between the two 1" PVC pipes. Cut two pieces of 1" PVC to a length that is about 2" longer than the distance between the pipes (see Figure 4). It is better to cut the pipe too long and trim a little later than to cut too short and have to start again.

5. Assemble the four 1" tees, the two pieces of 1" pipe you cut in the previous step, and the two 60" pieces of 1" pipe that slide inside the 1 ¼" PVC in the tire as shown in Figure 5. Check your work by

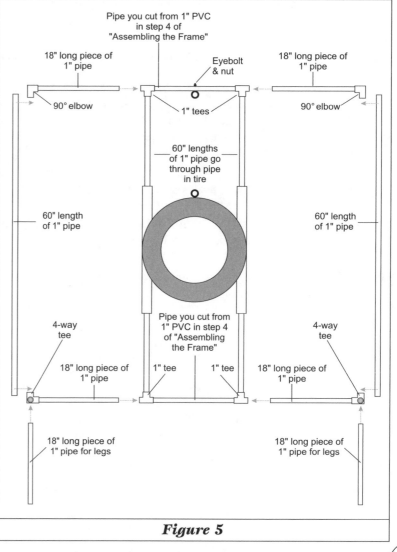

Figure 5

sliding the tire up and down from one set of tee joints to the other. When you are satisfied, disassemble the pipes and tees and then glue them back together.

6. Take two of the 18" pieces of 1" pipe and glue a 90° elbow on *one* end of each piece. Insert the opposite ends of the pipes into the tees at the top of the frame assembly as shown in Figure 5. Make sure they are lined up so that the open ends of the elbows face the ground and then glue them in place. It might help to insert two long pieces of PVC and use a level to make sure these elbows are aligned correctly before gluing them.

7. Take two more 18" pieces of 1" pipe and glue a 4-way tee on *one* end of each piece. Insert the opposite ends of the pipes into the tees at the bottom of the frame assembly as illustrated and glue.

8. When the glue has dried, bend the elbow and 4-way tee apart slightly and glue the last two pieces of 60" long 1" pipe in place as shown in Figure 5.

9. Insert an 18" piece of 1" pipe into the two remaining holes in each of the 4-way tees at the bottom of the frame. These are the stabilizing legs for the tire frame.

Mounting the Tire

1. When the glue is dry, drill a $1/4$" hole vertically through the center of the top piece of the frame (see Figure 5). Insert an eyebolt in this hole with the eye toward the tire and secure with a hex nut.

2. Mount a snap hook on this eyebolt and mount a breakable chain link on the eyebolt in the top of the tire. Link the plastic chain between the two.

3. Check the height of the tire by measuring from the bottom inside edge of the tire to the ground. Adjust the tire to one of the jump heights you will use and mark the appropriate chain link with ab piece of colored tape, nail polish, or paint. Repeat the process and mark the other links that you will use most.

*e*asily adjustable competition tire

this tire is fairly simple to make, but you will need to invest a lot of time in the initial "calibration" necessary to get the jump heights set up correctly. However, after this initial investment, it's easy to change heights, even during the heat of competition. The estimated cost to build this tire jump is $60.

Materials Needed

- 3 – 10' lengths 1 $1/2$" schedule 40 PVC
- 2 – 1 $1/2$" PVC 90° elbows
- 2 – 1 $1/2$" PVC 4-way tees

  NOTE: The 4-way tees are a special part not found in home centers or plumbing supply stores. They must be ordered from one of the vendors listed in the "Resource Guide" at the beginning of this book under "Furniture-Grade PVC Pipe and Parts." If you prefer not to order the 4-way tees, you can substitute *four* 1 $1/2$" PVC standard plumbing tees as described in "(Optional) Making a 4-Way Tee Substitute" on page 60.

- 4 – 1 $1/2$" PVC end caps
- 1 – 10' length 4" drain pipe, black plastic (with or without drain slits)
- 1 – internal connector for drain pipe

  NOTE: Some people are reporting that these are difficult to find. The external connectors make a large ridge in the tire which I find ugly, but you can use them in a pinch.

- 1 – 12" length of Tygon tubing, $1/4$" i.d.
- 20 – $1/4$" x 4" eyebolts (*not* eye screws)
- 20 – $1/4$" hex nuts

  NOTE: Be sure to count the nuts that come with the eyebolts so that you don't buy more hex nuts than you need.

- 12 – $1/4$" wing nuts
- 4 – $1/4$" fender washers
- 4 – $1/4$" toggle bolts
- 1 – package of $3/8$" polyester rope, 50' long

  NOTE: Polyester rope is difficult to find. Manila or sisal are good substitutes, but any other rope type is *not* a good substitute and will quickly rot if left outdoors. Be sure to get poly<u>ester</u> and *not* poly<u>propylene</u>.

- 2 – 40" long bungee cords

  NOTE: The stated length of bungee cords has nothing to do with their actual length. The ones labeled 40" are generally the longest available, which is what you want.

- 2 – 2" breakable chain links, also called repair links
- 2 – rope clamps

  NOTE: These can be the clamp-on type or the kind which use a U-bolt to make a strong loop out of the rope.

- 1 – roll silver duct tape
- 1 – roll colored plastic tape
- String
- 3 – spray cans of expanding foam insulation (optional)
- PVC cement
- 1 – sheet of 1" tall black press-on numbers

Tools Needed

- PVC cutter
- Hacksaw or Dremel tool with cutting wheel
- Scissors
- Razor blade or utility knife
- Drill with $1/4$" and $3/4$" bits
- Carpenter's level, preferably 3' long
- Carpenter's ruler or tape measure
- Pencil or marker
- Goggles or safety glasses
- Matches or a soldering iron
- Bucket of water

Cutting the PVC

Cut the following pieces from the 1 $1/2$" PVC:

2 – 60" long
2 – 48" long
4 – 12" long

(Optional) Making a 4-Way Tee Substitute

If you decided to use standard plumbing tees to construct your tire frame, follow the steps below. If you purchased 4-way tees, then skip to the next section, "Assembling the Tire Frame."

1. Cut two 3" long pieces of 1 $1/2$" PVC.

2. Put together two assemblies like those shown in Figure 1 by connecting two tees with a 3" piece of PVC. Do *not* glue anything yet. Put a 60" piece of PVC in the vertical mouth of the tee that points straight up. Then, use the level to make sure it is straight up and down.

3. Once you're sure that everything is properly aligned, glue each end of the 3" pieces into the tees. Do *not* glue the 60" piece in place.

Substitute these special parts you have made for the 4-way tees called for in the following sections.

Assembling the Tire Frame

1. Assemble the vertical sides of the tire frame first. For each 60" long piece of PVC, glue a 4-way tee on one end and a 90° elbow on the other end. If you glue the 4-way tee on before the elbow, it's easier. Before the glue dries, lay the pipe down on a flat surface so that the horizontal "mouth" of the 4-way tee (see Figure 2) is exactly parallel to the horizontal mouth of the elbow.

   NOTE: You can insert pieces of scrap PVC in the horizontal holes to help you get things lined up, but be sure not to glue them in.

2. Join the vertical sides with the two 48" pieces of PVC and glue as shown in Figure 3.

3. Glue an end cap onto each of the 12" pieces and then glue a 12" leg in each of the remaining holes in the 4-way tees.

Modifying the Eyebolts

Four of the eyebolts need to be modified so that you can slip a rope or bungee cord through them.

1. Each eyebolt is made from one continuous piece of steel wire. There is an end tucked up next to itself where the round part of the eyebolt curves around to meet itself. Using a hacksaw or a Dremel tool with a cutting wheel, remove about $1/4$" of the end to open a gap in the circle as shown in Figure 4. Be sure to wear goggles or safety glasses when you do this! Repeat to cut three more eyebolts.

2. Check each eyebolt to make sure that the rope and bungee cord can slip through the gap you have made as shown in Figure 5. It's okay if it's a very tight fit (stretching the bungee will help it slip through the gap). If your work is like mine and there is a little variation in the width of the gaps, line up the four modified eyebolts from smallest to largest gap. The two eyebolts with the narrower gaps can be used for the rope (upper) eyebolts and the two with the wider gaps can be used for the lower (bungee) eyebolts.

Attaching Mounting Hardware to the Frame

1. Working from the inside of the bottom part of the tire frame, drill a $1/4$" hole through the top of each 4-way tee where it meets the 60" vertical pipe. Drill all the way through from the inside to the outside of the frame as shown in Figure 6. Try to make these holes exactly parallel to the ground.

2. Insert one of the modified eyebolts into each hole with the eye on the inside of the frame and the threaded end sticking out on the

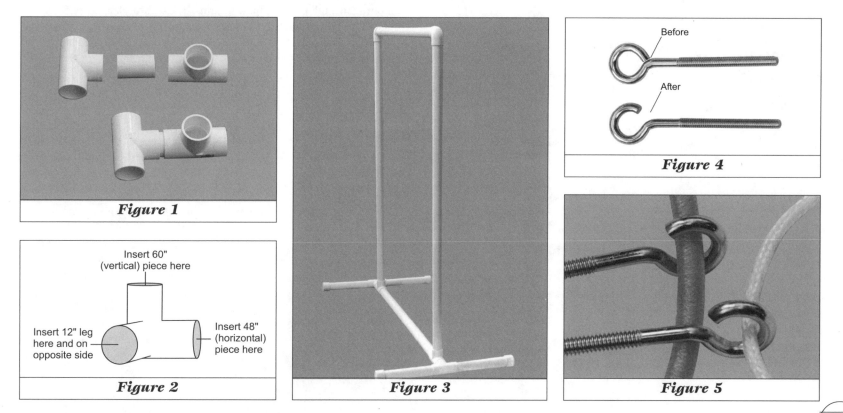

Figure 1

Insert 60" (vertical) piece here

Insert 12" leg here and on opposite side

Insert 48" (horizontal) piece here

Figure 2

Figure 3

Before

After

Figure 4

Figure 5

outside of the frame. Add a nut and tighten it securely. The gap on the eyebolt should point down toward the ground.

3. Working from the inside of the top part of the tire frame, drill a $1/4$" hole that goes diagonally from the inside corner of each 90° elbow to the outside corner as shown in Figure 6.

4. Insert one of the modified eyebolts into each hole you made with the eye on the inside of the frame and the threaded end sticking outward. Tighten the nuts just enough to hold the eyebolts in place. You need to leave them loose enough so that you can slip the rope through them in a later step.

Making the Tire

1. Cut the drain pipe to the length that you want. For a medium-sized USDAA tire (19" inner diameter), cut the drain pipe to 82". For an AKC tire (24" diameter), cut the pipe to 92".

2. Put the connector in one end of the cut drain pipe. Rip off four small pieces of duct tape. Divide the length of the drain pipe by 4. Measure this distance, starting 3" from the end of the pipe with the connector. Use a piece of tape to mark each position. For example, for an 82" piece of pipe, dividing by 4 gives you 20 $1/2$". You would mark the pipe in increments of 20 $1/2$", starting at 3". So you would put tape at 3", 23 $1/2$", 44", and 64 $1/2$".

3. Assemble the tire. Warning! Once you click the connector into place, there is no turning back. Bend the pipe around until it meets the connector, take a deep breath, and click it into place. It will be lopsided, but don't despair! Roll the "proto-tire" around on a hard, flat surface and push where it's too long. Rotate and push again. Continue rolling and pushing until you have a nice, round tire.

4. Mount four eyebolts on the tire. Drill $3/4$" holes in the sides of the drain pipe where you made the four marks. One of the holes should go through the connector; this helps hold everything together. A piece of plastic from each drill hole will fall down inside the tire. Shake them out through the drill hole now or they will rattle around and drive you nuts later!

5. Remove the threaded bolts from the toggle bolts you purchased and discard them. You only need the spring-loaded toggle "nut." Slip a fender washer on an eyebolt and then screw on a toggle so that it folds up toward the eye (see Figure 7). Turn the toggle nut so that it catches on the threads, but leave space between the arms of the toggle and the washer. Push the assembly into the $3/4$" hole and turn the eyebolt clockwise until it tightens inside the tire. Repeat to mount the other three eyebolts to the tire.

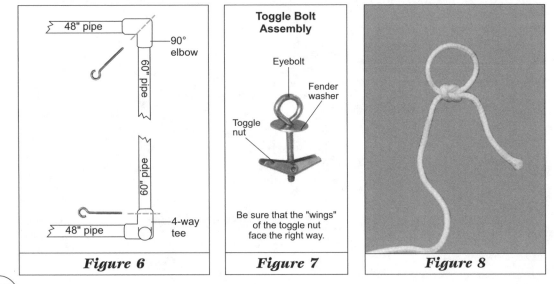

Toggle Bolt Assembly

Eyebolt

Fender washer

Toggle nut

Be sure that the "wings" of the toggle nut face the right way.

48" pipe

90° elbow

60" pipe

60" pipe

60" pipe

48" pipe

4-way tee

Figure 6

Figure 7

Figure 8

6. (Optional) To help keep the shape of the tire, you can fill it with expanding foam insulation. Using the ³/₄" bit, drill an extra four holes in the side of the tire. Lay the tire on a flat surface, open a can of expanding foam insulation, screw on the nozzle pipe, and let 'er rip into each hole. Be sure to point the nozzle in both directions through each hole. Note that the foam continues to expand during the first few minutes. It takes about 2 ¹/₄ cans to fill an AKC tire; a little less to fill a USDAA tire. Let the foam set overnight before proceeding. If any leaks out, cut away the excess with a utility knife.

7. Wrap the tire with duct tape. Start about midway between two eyebolts with the tape at a slight angle so that you're wrapping in a continuous spiral. When you get to an eyebolt, try to make the middle of the tape end up straddling the bolt. Turn it parallel to the length of the tape, cut a small slit in the tape so that it slips over the eye, and then rotate the eye back into place. After you've put on a roll of duct tape, wrap the tire with the colored tape. Be sure to make some contrasting stripes so that the dog can easily see the tire. You can use a contrasting color or put another band of silver duct tape on top of the plastic.

NOTE: Wrapping uses a lot of duct tape, which is expensive. However, I've found that buying cheap tape is false economy; only major brands last outside for any length of time. I use a base layer of silver cloth duct tape (I prefer 3M) and then overlay that with colored plastic tape from Industrial Safety, which holds up better than cloth duct tape. Even so, your tire will need rewrapping every year or so.

Preparing the Ropes and Bungee Cords

1. Measure out 78" of polyester rope and wrap a strip of plastic tape around the rope at this spot. Cut through the tape and rope with a utility knife or razor blade.

2. Get a bucket of water and some matches or a soldering iron. Carefully melt the ends of the rope to seal them so that they won't unravel. If the rope catches fire, dunk it in the water.

3. Loop the rope back on itself at each end so that the total length is about 67". Tie knots in the rope to form the loops. (I used two half-hitch knots which are similar to a square knot, but you don't need perfect knots.) Each loop should be about 1 ¹/₂"-2" long and big enough to slip over the top of an eyebolt as shown in Figure 8. Attach a rope clamp to one of the loose ends of the rope as in Figure 9.

4. Repeat steps 1-3 to prepare a second length of rope.

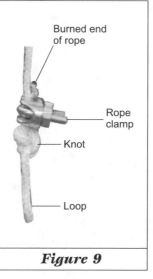

Burned end of rope

Rope clamp

Knot

Loop

Figure 9

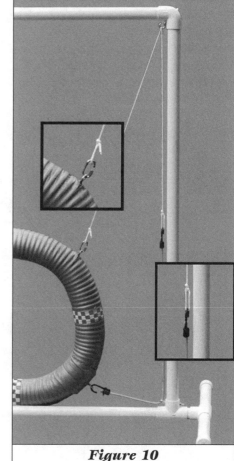

Figure 10

5. Slip a rope into the gap in one of the eyebolts at the top of the tire frame (the ones in the 90° elbows). Repeat for the other side. Tighten the nuts securely. The rope should be trapped inside the eyebolt.

6. Slip a bungee cord in to the gap in one of the eyebolts at the bottom of the tire frame (the ones in the 4-way tees). Repeat for the other side.

7. Using scissors, cut four 1"-2" long pieces of Tygon tubing. Push a piece of the tubing onto the protruding threads of the eyebolts at the top and bottom of the tire frame so that no sharp edges remain.

8. Get the tire and stand it up on the ground inside the center of the frame. Using the two breakable links, attach each eyebolt sticking out of the top part of the tire to the loop without the rope clamp in each rope, left and right, as shown in Figure 10.

9. Attach one end of a bungee cord to each of the eyebolts sticking out of the bottom of the tire, left and right. Make sure the bungee cord is still hooked on the bottom eyebolt attached to the tire frame and then join the free hook on the bungee to the free loop on each rope (the one with the rope clamp), left and right, as shown in Figure 10. You should need to stretch the bungee cord a bit to attach it, but don't exert yourself. If the rope is too short, you will need to go back and tie a longer one for each side. If the rope is too long, you can either tie a shorter one or you can tie knots in the bungee to shorten it.

NOTE: the length of the rope will vary, depending on the size of the tire and the length of the bungees you've bought. The numbers in step 3 are a general guide, but will vary depending on your construction. What's important is that there is a bit of tension in both bungees when they are connected to the rope loops.

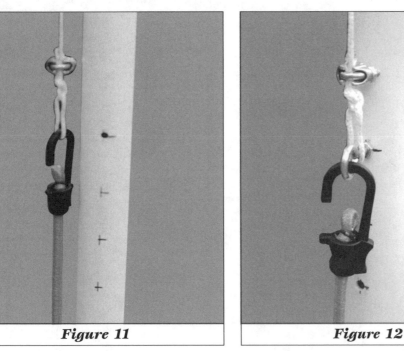

| Figure 11 | Figure 12 |

jumps and hurdles

Hanging the Tire

1. Step back and make sure the tire is centered in the frame. Note that you can slide the tire up and down to set its height, but there is (as yet) no way to keep it in place.

2. Slide the tire so that it is gently resting on the ground as in Figure 10. Make a mark on the front surface of the left vertical pipe of the frame where the rope and the hook on the bungee cord meet. Repeat on the front surface of the right vertical pipe of the frame. Measuring from the ground up, make sure the marks are the same distance from the ground. If not, take the average and mark the vertical pipes appropriately.

3. Starting with the mark you just made, measure down 2" and make another mark. Continue marking the vertical pipe at 2" intervals until you are about 6" from the ground. Using the level, make a vertical line that intersects each mark. Repeat for the other side of the frame.

4. Using the $1/4$" bit, drill a hole through each of the marks you just made as shown in Figure 11. You will be drilling from the front of each vertical pipe through to the back side.

5. Screw a hex nut onto a eyebolt. Keep tightening it until you reach the end of the threads near the "eye." Repeat for each of the other remaining hex nuts.

6. Insert one of the eyebolts you just prepared in each hole you drilled in the tire frame as shown in Figure 12. The eyes should be toward the front of the frame and the threads of the bolts should be pointing outward to the back of the frame. Secure the back of each bolt in place with a wing nut.

Calibrate the Tire Height

1. Again, step back and make sure the tire is centered side to side within the frame. Then, use a tape measure to judge the distance between the bottom of the tire aperture and the ground. If this is an "official" height, mark the height next to the eyebolt in the frame. Repeat until all "official" heights are marked. Remember that the higher the bolt, the lower the tire. Also remember that all organizations allow some tolerance in the measurement (generally $1/2$" above or below the stated jump height). With the eyebolts at 2" intervals, you should be able to find settings for all the jump heights you need. If not, you can drill an additional hole halfway between any two holes.

2. Add a press-on number representing the jump height next to each of the holes on one or both of the vertical pipes. Again, note that the setting for the lowest jump height will be furthest above the ground, and vice versa.

3. To change jump heights, release the bungee cords where they attach to the frame. Then, with one hand, support the tire, and use the other hand to slip both ropes free from the frame. Lift or lower the tire to its new height, use your free hand to slip the ropes over the corresponding eyebolts mounted on the tire frame, and replace the bungees in the same eyebolt that holds the rope.

Plastic broad jump with built-in marking poles

the broad jump is a required obstacle in AKC Novice agility competition and is an obstacle sometimes seen in other levels of AKC competition as well as in USDAA competition where it's often referred to as the long jump. (Broad jumps are not used in NADAC.)

Before you begin, decide which style of agility you want the jump for. AKC agility rules specify up to four broad jump boards, while USDAA rules specify up to five. If you're using the jump for training at home, you may want to make only enough boards for the span your dog jumps.

In AKC, the jump width (span) is twice the dog's jump height except in 4" height division of the Preferred class where the broad jump is set as only one board (the lowest).

Generally, you use as many boards as fit within the span.

AKC Broad Jump		USDAA Long Jump	
Height Division	**Broad Jump Span**	**Height Division**	**Broad Jump Span**
8"	16"	12"	20"
12"	24"	16"	36"
16"	32"	22"	48"
20"	40"	26"	60"
24"	48"		

Materials Needed

The following materials list is for making five jump boards. Reduce the amounts if you don't need or want a complete USDAA (60" jump span) set. Each 10' piece of PVC pipe will make one jump board. Two 10' pieces are needed for the marker poles.

- 7 – 10' lengths ¹/₂" schedule 40 PVC
- 30 – ¹/₂" PVC 90° elbows
- 10 – ¹/₂" PVC tees
- 4 – ¹/₂" PVC end caps

- 2 – 8" wide x 12' long vinyl fascia boards (vinyl siding) shaped as shown in Figure 1

  NOTE: Home center employees will swear they don't carry this, but they do! Keep asking until you get what you want.

- 25 – #6 x 1" drywall screws
- PVC cement

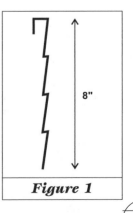

Figure 1

Tools Needed

- Dremel tool (preferred) or hacksaw
- Scissors-type PVC cutters
- Drill with ³/₆₄" bit
- Carpenter's ruler or tape measure
- Pencil or marker

Making the Front (Lowest) Board

1. Using a Dremel tool or hacksaw, remove ¹/₂" from one end of four PVC 90° elbows as shown in Figure 2. Also remove ¹/₂" from one end of two PVC tees. It doesn't matter which end of the elbow you cut off, but it *does* matter which end of the tee you cut—you want to cut one of the ends on the "long" side of the tee as shown.

   NOTE: You are making these "special" tees and elbows for the lowest board supports. If you don't cut this material away, the board will not be short enough.

2. Cut the following pieces from a 10' length of PVC:

   2 – 46" long
   2 – 5 ¹/₂" long
   4 – 1" long

3. Make a right and left front corner assembly. These assemblies should be mirror images. Put each one together using a cut tee, a 1" piece of pipe, and a cut 90° elbow as illustrated in Figure 3. Notice how the elbow is twisted so that it points upward while the tee is facing sideways. Check to see that the distance from the top of one arm of the tee to the bottom of the open end of the elbow is 2 ¹/₂" for both assemblies. If not, recut the PVC pieces as needed.

NOTE: Practice getting the tee and elbow at a right angle to each other. I rest the assembly on the open end of the elbow on my workbench and then check that the arm of the tee is parallel to the bench. It helps to put a scrap piece of PVC in the tee so that you can see what is going on. When you've practiced as much as you can stand, begin gluing together the left and right front corner assemblies.

4. Make a right and left rear corner assembly by pairing uncut elbows with cut elbows as in Figure 4. Again, assemble the parts and measure these assemblies before gluing. The top-to-bottom measurement should be 3" as shown. If it's not, recut the PVC pieces as needed.

5. Join the left front and left rear assemblies and the right front and right rear assemblies with a 5 ¹/₂" piece of PVC pipe as in Figure 5. Again, make sure everything lines up, and then glue.

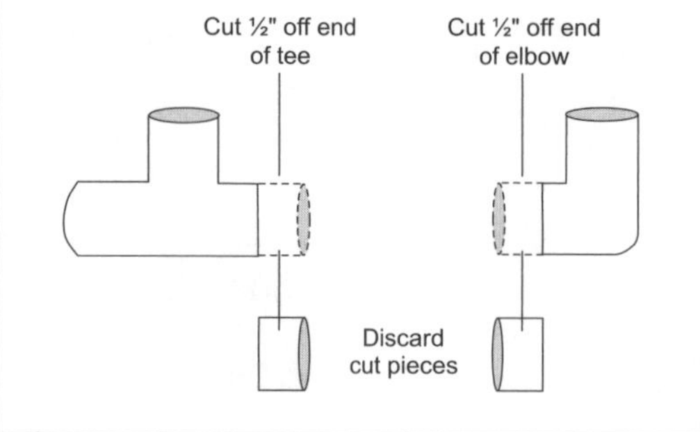

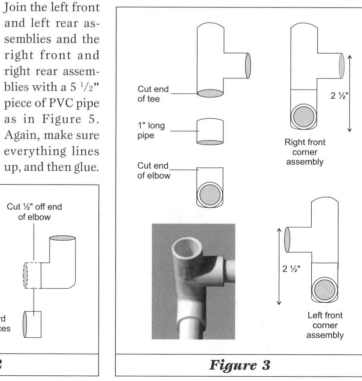

Cut end of tee

1" long pipe

Cut end of elbow

2 ½"

Right front corner assembly

2 ½"

Left front corner assembly

Cut ½" off end of tee

Cut ½" off end of elbow

Discard cut pieces

Figure 2

Figure 3

6. Join the left side of the board with the right side using the 46" pieces of pipe. Before gluing, make sure the two sides line up and form a base that will rest flat without rocking. Figure 6 shows the completed front board skeleton before the fascia board is added.

7. Cut the 12' length of vinyl siding (fascia) into three 48" lengths with a Dremel tool or hacksaw. There will be some left over because the vinyl siding is a little longer than 12'.

8. Cut four corners off the siding with a Dremel tool or hacksaw as shown in Figure 7.

9. Mount the fascia board onto the skeleton. Slip the U-shaped part of the fascia board over the rear (higher) 46" pipe, then drill four or five pilot holes through the siding and into the pipe. The open ends of the tees, at the front of the jump board, will be the sockets that the marker poles will be inserted into. Use drywall screws to attach the fascia board to the skeleton. Put the screws in the backside of the jump to eliminate the risk of a dog getting a pad torn if he nicks the jump.

Making the Center and Back Boards

Assembly of the three (AKC) or four (USDAA) center/back boards is basically the same, with a few exceptions.

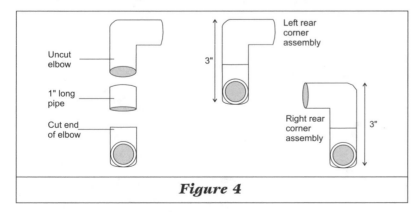

Figure 4

- You do not need to cut any of the PVC elbows or tees.
- The tees will form part of the back corner, *not* the front.
- You only need to clip the back corner of the fascia board, *not* the front.

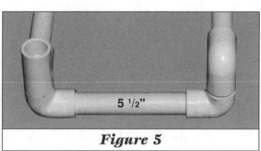

Figure 5

General instructions for assembly of the center and back boards are given here. All of the boards are assembled in the same way, but use different lengths of PVC for the front and rear corner pieces.

1. Cut two 5 1/2" lengths of pipe and two 46" lengths of pipe for each jump board you want to make.

2. Cut the pieces of PVC that you will need to make the front and rear corner assemblies for each board using the information in the table below.

   NOTE: As you cut the pipe, it's a good idea to mark (in pencil) the length of each piece of pipe on it so that you don't get confused.

Height of front edge of board	Height of back edge of board	Cut two pieces of PVC pipe to this length	Cut two pieces of PVC pipe to this length
3 1/2"	4"	1"	1 1/2"
4 1/2"	5"	2"	2 1/2"
5 1/2"	6"	3"	3 1/2"
6 1/2" (USDAA only)	7"	4"	4 1/2"

3. Taking the longer pieces of pipe, assemble a left and right rear corner for each board using a tee and an elbow. Use Figure 8 to guide you.

4. Taking the shorter pieces of pipe, assemble a left and right front corner for each board using two 90° elbows. Use Figure 8 to guide you.

5. Assemble the left side of each board by joining both left assemblies with a 5 ¹/₂" piece of pipe. Do the same for the right side. Then, again being careful to make sure everything is flat and square before gluing, join the right and left assemblies with 46" pieces of pipe. This completes the jump board skeleton.

6. Cut the remaining 12' length of vinyl siding (fascia) into three 48" lengths with a Dremel tool or hacksaw.

7. Cut two corners off the U-shaped side of the fascia board. This will accommodate the upright part of the tee as shown in Figure 9.

8. Mount the fascia board onto the skeletons you assembled. Slip the U-shaped part of each fascia board over the rear (higher) 46" pipe. then drill four or five pilot holes through the siding and into the pipe. Use drywall screws to attach the fascia boards to the skeletons.

Finishing the Boards

The ends of each board (a 3" to 4" section) need to be marked in a contrasting color if you want to use these for competition. Paint does not stick to PVC so I use colored duct tape or plastic tape to mark the boards.

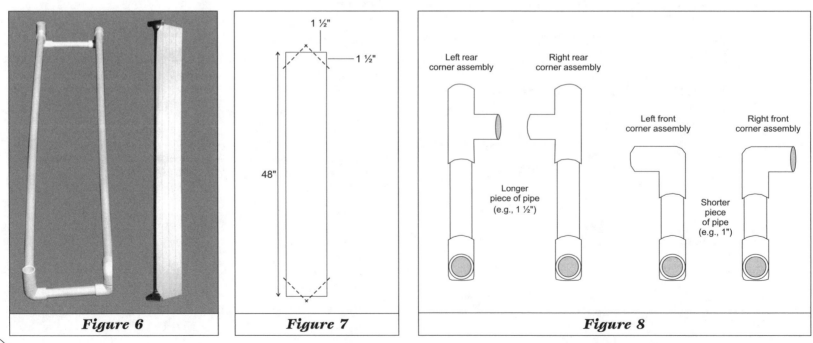

Figure 6   *Figure 7*   *Figure 8*

Making the Marker Poles

The marker poles fit into the front tees of the shortest board and into the back tees of whatever the tallest board is of the four or five you made.

1. Cut the last two pieces of 10' PVC into four 40" lengths.

2. Glue an end cap to one side of each of the four pieces of pipe. The other end will be inserted into the tees that are built in to the boards.

   NOTE: Do *not* glue the marker poles in place or you won't be able to move them from one board to another to accommodate different jump heights. The front pair of marker poles stays with the short board, while the back pair of marker poles moves to whichever board is being used.

Figure 9

Wooden broad jump with marking poles

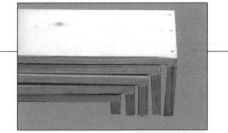

the broad jump built from these plans can be used for obedience practice as well. However, if you want a regulation AKC obedience broad jump, you must paint it plain white. The painting scheme suggested in the steps that follow is for an agility broad jump.

If you have a small dog and you only want a broad jump for practice, then you do not need to build all of the boards. For example, dogs jumping 8" in AKC or USDAA need only boards A and B in the table below and so forth.

AKC Agility Broad Jump

Dog's Jump Height	Broad Jump Width	Boards Needed
4"		A
8"	16"	A + B
12"	24"	A + B + C
16"	32"	A + B + C
20"	40"	A + B + C + D
24"	48"	A + B + C + D

AKC Obedience Broad Jump

Dog's Jump Height	Broad Jump Width	Boards Needed
8" to 12"	16" to 24"	A + B
14" to 22"	28" to 44"	A + B + C
24" to 36"	48" to 72"	A + B + C + D

USDAA Long Jump

Dog's Jump Height	Broad Jump Width	Boards Needed
8"	12"	A + B*
12"	20"	A + B
16"	36"	A + B + C + D
22"	48"	A + B + C + D + E
26"	60"	A + B + C + D + E

*   For dogs in the USDAA 12" Performance division, you must build the broad jump using 1x6 lumber instead of 1x8.

These plans are organized in two parts:

- Making the broad jump boards—Follow these steps regardless of whether you are making an AKC agility or obedience broad jump or a USDAA long jump.

- Making marker poles—Follow the set of steps appropriate for the type of marker poles you want for your broad jump. Using $3/4$" PVC produces marker poles that are sleek, but not very easy to move. Using 1 $1/4$" PVC makes big, "clunky" looking marker poles that are easily moved to accommodate different jump heights.

Making the Broad Jump Boards

Materials Needed

- 1" x 8" x 6' boards

  NOTE: Use the table to determine how many boards you need, or buy five boards for a full set.

- 1 – box 1 $1/2$" or 1 $5/8$" exterior, fine-thread drywall screws

- Paint (white and one other color for an agility broad jump)

- 1 – roll masking tape

Tools Needed

- Circular saw or table saw
- Carpenter's square
- Spring clamps or C-clamps
- Drill with $1/8$" bit and Philips head bit
- Carpenter's ruler or tape measure
- Pencil or marker

1. Using a circular saw or tablesaw, cut the boards to the lengths indicated in Figure 1. The shorter pieces to the right of each broad jump board in the diagram will be used to make the supports for that particular board.

NOTE: Measure and mark each board carefully; you want to make your first cuts very close to 90° to the side of the board, especially on the shorter boards. If you use a carpenter's square and follow your pencil marks scrupulously, you will save time in the long run. There will be some left over so, if necessary, you can recut the shorter boards until you get a good rectangular piece.

2. Cut the shorter boards as shown in Figure 2. Measure each side of the board, then make two marks and connect them with a line. For example, for the supports for board A, mark 1" from one end at the top of the board, 1" from the opposite end at the bottom of the board, and draw a diagonal line to connect them. Even if you're off a bit, as long as your cut in step 1 was perpendicular, the angle at each end of the support will be the same. Geometry in action! After you have cut each set of supports, stack them together to make sure they match perfectly. If they do not, you can clamp them together and recut them (I prefer this method) or cut another set until you have two that are a match.

3. On each of the long boards, draw two lines. Each line should be parallel to the side of the board and *exactly* $3/8$" from the end as shown in Figure 3. Repeat for the other end of the board. Check your measurements several times as you will use this line to guide your drill holes into the jump supports.

4. Assemble each of your long jump boards as shown in Figures 4 and 5. Place the two supports for the board about 5' apart on a flat surface with the angled surface facing up. Then, place the long, horizon-

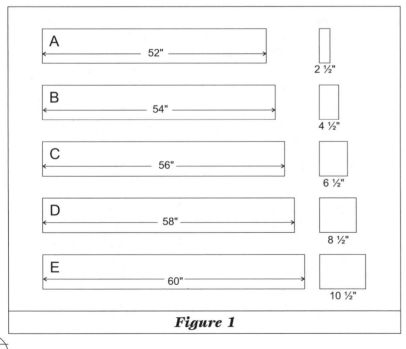

Figure 1

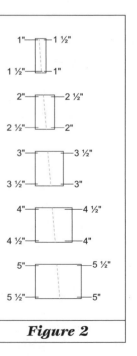

Figure 2

tal board on top of the supports. Move the supports in or out until they are flush with the edges of the top board. If you have corner clamps around, now is the time to use them. When everything is lined up, hold the assembly tight and drill three pilot holes from the top of the long board into the supports. Drive drywall screws through the pilot holes.

5. Before painting, see Figure 6. Note that a contrasting stripe is required for an agility broad jump; you can either paint the center white and the sides a contrasting color, or the center colored and the sides a contrasting white. Paint a white primer coat on every piece. When the primer coat is completely dry, mask off two parallel lines about 6-12" from each end. Apply a second coat of a contrasting color either inside or outside these masked lines. When the color coat is dry, move the tape to line up with the edge of the colored area and repaint the white areas.

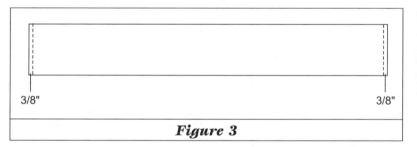

3/8"   3/8"

Figure 3

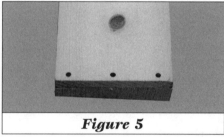

Figure 5

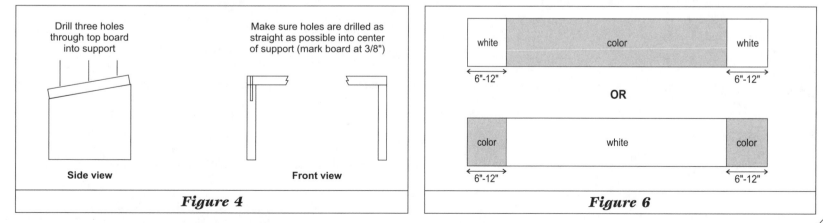

Drill three holes
through top board
into support

Make sure holes are drilled as
straight as possible into center
of support (mark board at 3/8")

Side view   **Front view**

Figure 4

white | color | white
6"-12"   6"-12"

OR

color | white | color
6"-12"   6"-12"

Figure 6

Making Marker Poles: ³/₄" PVC

Materials Needed

- 2 – 10' lengths ³/₄" schedule 40 PVC
- 4 – ³/₄" schedule 40 PVC end caps
- 1 – package Fibermax rod posts (Jeffers Equine, part #F8-R1-13)
- PVC cement

Tools Needed

- Scissors-type PVC cutters
- Sledgehammer
- Carpenter's ruler or tape measure
- Pencil or marker

Directions

1. Cut four pieces of PVC, each 48" long.
2. Glue an end cap on one end of each cut piece.
3. Measure and set the broad jump, then pound Fibermax rod posts into the ground, one for each corner. Slip a piece of PVC with an end cap over each rod post.

Making Marker Poles: 1 ¹/₄" PVC

Materials Needed

- 2 – 10' lengths 1 ¹/₄" schedule 40 PVC
- 4 – 1 ¹/₄" schedule 40 PVC end caps

- 1 – package of 10 Dare Step-In Posts (Jeffers Equine part #D4-S7-13)
- 1 – bag multicolored golf tees

Tools Needed

- Scissors-type PVC cutters
- Sledgehammer
- Dremel tool (preferred) or hacksaw
- Carpenter's ruler or tape measure
- Pencil or marker

Directions

1. Cut four pieces of PVC, each 48" long.
2. Glue an end cap on one end of each cut piece.
3. Each Dare Step-In Post has approximately eight hooks for attaching fence wire and a square top. These are fine for fences, but they are in your way. The PVC pipe will not fit over the fence post unless you remove them. Using the Dremel tool or a hacksaw, cut off these hooks and the square top.
4. Slip a piece of PVC with an end cap over the stripped Dare fence post until a tight fit is obtained. This will make a stick-in-the-ground marker post, which can be easily moved from place to place.

   TIP: When setting the broad jump for multiple jump heights, decide which pair of marker poles will stay in place and which will move. (AKC requires that the shorter boards be fixed and the longer boards move.) Then, measure the distance from the fixed pair of poles and mark these with golf tees. When changing jump heights, move the other pair of posts to the new location, as marked by the tees, and shift the jump to fit within the rectangle created by the four posts.

Chapter two

Tunnels and Accessories

agility tunnels can be of two types:

- Open or pipe tunnel
- Closed or collapsed tunnel

Buying an Open Tunnel

The open or pipe tunnel is a flexible tube that's approximately 24" wide and anywhere from 10' to 20' in length. Pipe tunnels for competition need to be purchased from a commercial source. You cannot make one. A list is provided in the "Resource Guide" at the beginning of this book.

For the backyard agility enthusiast on a budget, a fabric tunnel from a toy store will serve your needs. There is also a list of suppliers of fabric tunnels in the "Resource Guide."

If you are purchasing an open tunnel to be used in competition, you should keep the following regulations for the different organizations in mind:

- AKC—The two openings must be round with a height and width of 24" (plus or minus 2" allowed) and a length of 10'-20'. Open tunnels must be made of an opaque material. To ensure safety, the color of the material may *not* be black. If the tunnel is double lined, dark interiors such as dark blue, dark brown, dark green, dark red/burgundy, and dark purple are *not* allowed.

- NADAC/ASCA—The diameter should be 24" and the length should be 10'-20'.

- USDAA—The diameter should be approximately 24" and the length should be no less than 10' and no more than 20'. The spacing between the wires or supports that hold the tunnel material open (called the pitch) must be no more than 4".

Making a Closed Tunnel

The closed tunnel consists of a rigid opening and a fabric chute or "sleeve" through which the dog passes. There are several options for constructing the rigid opening and framework for the tunnel. The first set of plans in this chapter uses a lightweight PVC frame. The next set of plans is for a wooden frame shaped like a doghouse. The wooden design will make the tunnel heavier to move around than the PVC support, but you gain stability and the barrel will not slide. Like everything else in life, it's a tradeoff. You need to select the design that best suits how you will be using the tunnel. If you need a tunnel to withstand trial or class situations, you may want to build the one with a wooden frame.

Selecting a Barrel

The main component of your closed tunnel will be a plastic barrel. Cardboard drums are *not* recommended as they will not hold up to weather or time. The diameter of the barrel you select is dependent on the agility venue(s) for which you are training. AKC rules specify a rigid opening of 22"-26" in diameter, NADAC rules an opening of no less than 22 ½", and USDAA rules an opening of 18"-24". If you get a 23" diameter barrel for your collapsed tunnel, it will work for all three venues. However, if you want your dog to get used to squeezing through a smaller opening, you might want an 18 ½" diameter barrel.

Commercial barrels for industrial use, usually referred to as drums, come in standard sizes. When you are selecting a drum, use the following guidelines:

- 30-gallon drum—18 ½" inside diameter
- 35-gallon drum—20 ¼" inside diameter
- 55-gallon drum—23" inside diameter

Plastic barrels are available free of charge from most car washes. If you get a detergent barrel from a car wash, rinse it thoroughly before using it. Under *no* circumstances use a barrel that has contained toxic or hazardous material such as pesticides.

If you are concerned about the source of your barrel, it's best to purchase a new one that's never been used. U.S. Plastics (USP) sells barrels in various groovy colors, which is important since you can't paint plastic. The ones with molded-in tops (closed-head) are slightly cheaper, but require much more cutting. USP catalog numbers for open-head (removable top) drums are as follows:

- 30 gallon: #74153 red, #74158 white, #74163 blue, #74168 black, #74173 yellow, or #74178 green.
- 35 gallon: #74154 red, #74159 white, #74164 blue, #74169 black, #74174 yellow, or #74179 green.
- 55 gallon: #74155 red, #74160 white, #74165 blue, #74170 black, #74175 yellow, or #74180 green.

You can also purchase colored plastic drums (both open-head and closed-head) from Global Equipment Company. Their prices are slightly higher than those of U.S. Plastics, but depending on where you live, you might save on shipping.

Buying or Making a Chute

You can buy a commercially-made chute for your closed tunnel or you can sew your own. If you wish to buy a chute, refer to the manufacturers listed in the "Resource Guide" at the beginning of the book. If you would like to try your hand at making a chute, you can use the plans included here.

Below are the specifications for the chute at the time of this writing. The circumference of the chute should flare from the circumference of the rigid opening to the "Flare To" Circumference noted for the exit. Note that AKC regulations specifiy the overall length of the closed tunnel should be 12'-15'. Therefore, the length of your chute depends on the length of the barrel you use for the opening section.

Organization	Length	"Flare To" Circumference
AKC	10'-12'	86"-90"
NADAC/ASCA	8'	96"
USDAA	12'	96"

NOTE: USDAA requires the fabric for the chute to be less than 6 ounces per square yard or 420 denier.

Plans Included

In this section, you will find the following plans:

- Closed Tunnel with PVC Frame
- Closed Tunnel with Wooden Doghouse Frame
- Fabric Chute for the Closed Tunnel

 losed tunnel with PVC frame

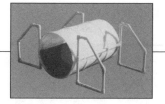

t his closed tunnel uses a lightweight PVC frame. You might want to weight the frame with sandbags or stake it down, especially if you have a dog that tends to rip through the closed tunnel.

Materials Needed

- 1 – plastic barrel
- 1 – doormat or piece of indoor-outdoor carpeting at least 24" x 36"
- 1 – tube Liquid Nails exterior adhesive caulk
- 3 – 10' lengths $^3/_4$" Schedule 40 PVC
- 8 – $^3/_4$" PVC 45° elbows
- 12 – $^3/_4$" PVC 90° elbows
- 4 – $^3/_4$" PVC tees
- PVC cement

If you cannot get them locally, the following items are available from Small Parts, Inc.

- 4 – nylon machine screws, binding head, $^1/_4$" x 2" (#Y-MN-1420-32-B)
- 4 – nylon nuts for machine screws (#Y-HNN-1420)
- 8 – nylon washers for screws (#Y-WN-1/4W)

Tools Needed

- Circular saw, Dremel tool, sabre saw, or band saw (best choice for this job)
- Piece of string
- Level or plumb bob
- Sandpaper
- Caulk gun
- Drill with $^1/_8$" and $^1/_4$" bits
- Scissors-type PVC cutting shears or saw
- Screwdriver for machine screws
- Wrench or socket for $^7/_{16}$" nut
- Carpenter's ruler or tape measure
- Pencil or marker

Preparing the Barrel

1. Cut off the bottom of the barrel (the end without the lid). To determine where to make this cut, you need to decide how long you want the barrel to be. For AKC, the barrel can be 24"-36" long. However, for NADAC and USDAA, the barrel cannot be longer than 30". Measure the length you want starting from the top of the barrel. At this point, tie a piece of string around the barrel and secure it with a tight knot. This will guide your cut. The fastest way to make the cut is to use a circular saw and have an assistant rotate the barrel for you. However, this is also the fastest way to cut off a limb. It's safer, but slower, to use a Dremel tool or sabre saw. (Be sure to lay in a good supply of cutting wheels or blades!)

NOTE: If you have a closed head barrel, the top of the barrel will have a lip, which is slightly larger than the rest. The bottom end is the opposite one.

2. If you have a closed head barrel, you need to cut out the top. Because you want to preserve the lip for attaching the fabric chute, you cannot just cut off the top end of the barrel as you did the bottom. Instead, you need to cut just *inside* the lip. To do this, you will first need to drill a pilot hole so that you can insert the saw through the top of the barrel.

3. Using sandpaper or a Dremel tool, smooth off the rough edges where the barrel end(s) were removed.

4. With the cut bottom end of the barrel facing up, make a mark anywhere along the top of the barrel. Then, measure carefully to find the widest point across the opening. Make a mark on the outside surface of the barrel at the center of this measurement as shown in Figure 1. Using a level or plumb bob, draw a straight line down the length of the barrel starting at the mark. Repeat for the opposite side of the barrel.

   NOTE: This is a good time to double-check the barrel's measurements to make sure it is legal for the type of agility you plan to do.

5. A nonskid surface for the part of the barrel that will be the bottom of the tunnel opening is required in most forms of agility. If you use exterior-rated adhesive caulk for this step, the job will last a long time. Cut a piece of indoor-outdoor carpeting or a floor mat to a width of 24" and a length that is as long as your barrel. Turn over the piece of carpeting or matting so that the backing (nonuseable) side faces you. With a caulk gun, spread a layer of adhesive exterior caulk over the entire surface. Use a putty knife or a scrap of wood to spread it evenly. Carefully pick up the piece of carpeting so that the two edges almost touch and place it inside the barrel, centering it between the two lines you made in step 4. Applying pressure, smooth down the carpeting so that it makes good contact with the inside surface of the barrel.

Making the PVC Frame

1. Cut the following pieces from the ³/₄" PVC:

   8 – 12" long
   4 – 8" long
   2 – 4" shorter than the length of your barrel (for example, 26" long for a 30" long barrel)
   4 – 3" long

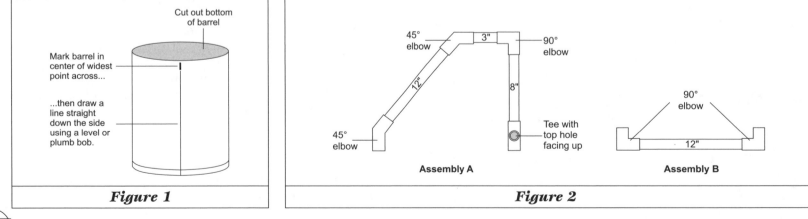

Figure 1

Figure 2

2. Put together four Assembly As and four Assembly Bs as shown in Figure 2. Do *not* glue yet. Make sure that everything fits together correctly. Check that each assembly lies flat by placing it on a work-bench or other surface and pressing so that everything is in place. Be sure that the tee on each Assembly A is facing straight up. It helps to insert a scrap piece of PVC pipe in the open hole (the hole facing you in the diagram) and then use a level to make sure the scrap PVC is straight.

3. Begin gluing together each assembly, working one joint at a time so that everything stays flat. When gluing together each Assembly A, save the tee for last and then check it again with a level before the glue sets.

4. Take one of the long PVC pieces you cut in step 1 and align it with one of the lines you marked on the side of the barrel as shown in Figure 3. The end of the pipe should be flush with the bottom, cut-out end of the barrel. This will leave approximately 4" between the other end of the pipe and the top, lipped end of the barrel. (You need to have enough room between the frame and the barrel top to attach the fabric chute later on.) Clamp the piece of pipe in place or have an assistant hold it. Drill two $\frac{1}{8}$" pilot holes through the PVC pipe and the barrel. Then switch to a $\frac{1}{4}$" bit and drill through the pilot holes to make them bigger. Repeat to attach the other long piece of PVC to the opposite side of the barrel.

5. Thread a washer onto a nylon bolt, then thread the bolt through one of the holes you just made. The head of the bolt should be in-side the barrel. (Nylon is used because it will not rot or rust out-doors, and there are no sharp edges to cut the dog.) Add another washer to the side of the bolt that sticks out from the PVC pipe and thread a nut onto this assembly until the threads catch. Don't tighten the assembly yet. Repeat for the other holes you drilled.

6. Lay the barrel on its side on a level surface as shown in Figure 4. Take one of the Assembly As you put together in step 2 and slip the open hole of the tee onto an end of one of the pipes bolted to the barrel. This will be the top of one of the four stabilizing "wings" that will hold the barrel upright. Take one of the Assembly B's you put together in step 2 and place it on your working surface directly below Assembly A with the open ends of the elbows pointing up. This will be the bottom of one of the stabilizing wings. Measure the

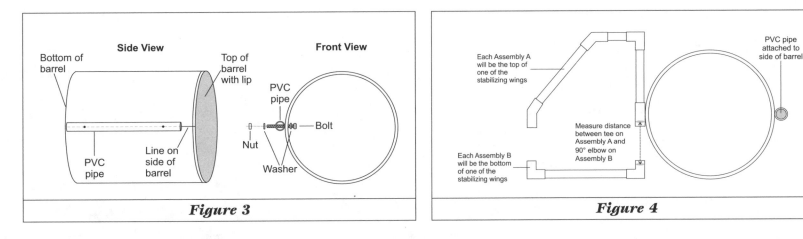

Figure 3

Figure 4

distance between the open (downward-pointing) end of the tee and the open (upward-pointing) end of the 90° elbow. Be sure to measure all the way to where the pipe will stop inside each PVC fitting. Cut eight pieces of PVC pipe to this length. (For example, for the 30-gallon barrel I used, these pieces were 8" long.)

7. Remove the assembly you were using for measuring from the pipe on the barrel. Assemble the four support wings using the pieces you cut in the previous step to join the top and bottom parts of each wing. Make sure everything fits properly. When you are satisfied that all is well, glue the wings together.

8. Slide a wing onto the end of each pipe on the barrel. Line up everything and then tighten the bolts you inserted in step 5. Glue on the wings.

Closed tunnel with wooden doghouse frame

t hese plans are for building a closed tunnel with a wooden doghouse-shaped frame.

Materials Needed

- 1 – 55-gallon plastic barrel (approx. 23 $^1/_2$" diameter)
- 1 – doormat or piece of indoor-outdoor carpeting at least 24" x 36"
- 1 – tube Liquid Nails exterior adhesive caulk
- 1 – 4' x 8' sheet of $^1/_2$" CDX plywood
- 3 – 2" x 4" x 8' framing lumber (studs)
- 1 – box #8 x 2" exterior drywall screws, fine thread
- 1 – box #8 x 3" exterior drywall screws, fine thread
- 1 – piece steel or aluminum roof ridge flashing, about 6" wide

  NOTE: This is a very thin strip of metal with a crease down the middle and is used to cover the seam where the two pieces of plywood meet at the top of the roof.

If you cannot get them locally, the following items are available from Small Parts, Inc.

- 4 – $^1/_4$" x 2" nylon binding head machine screws (#Y-MN-1420-32-B)
- 4 – nuts for machine screws (#Y-HNN-1420)
- 4 – washers for screws (#Y-WN-1/4W)

Tools Needed

- For cutting the barrel: circular saw, Dremel tool, sabre saw, or jig saw (best choice for this job)

- For cutting the doghouse front: jig saw
- For cutting the wood pieces: circular saw with adjustable angle blade
- Piece of string
- Level or plumb bob at least 30" long
- Sandpaper
- Caulk gun
- Drill with $^1/_{16}$", $^1/_4$", and $^1/_2$" bits
- Screwdriver for machine screws
- Wrench or socket for $^7/_{16}$" nut
- Hacksaw or Dremel tool to cut roof ridge flashing
- Carpenter's pencil
- Carpenter's ruler
- Tape measure
- (Optional, but useful) Spring-loaded clamps for wood projects, 4" grip range

Preparing the Barrel

1. Cut off the bottom of the barrel (the end without the lid). To determine where to make this cut, measure 36" down from the top of the barrel. At this point, tie a piece of string around the barrel and secure it with a tight knot. This will guide your cut. The fastest way

to make the cut is to use a circular saw and have an assistant rotate the barrel for you. However, this is also the fastest way to cut off a limb. It's safer, but slower, to use a Dremel tool or sabre saw. (Be sure to lay in a good supply of cutting wheels or blades!)

NOTE: If you have a closed-head barrel, the top of the barrel will have a lip. The bottom end is the opposite one.

2. If you have a closed-head barrel, you need to cut out the top. You want to preserve the lip for attaching the fabric chute, so you cannot just cut off the top of the barrel as you did the bottom. Instead, cut just *inside* the lip. To do this, you will first need to drill a pilot hole so that you can insert the saw through the top of the barrel.

3. Using sandpaper or a Dremel tool, smooth off the rough edges where the barrel end(s) were removed.

4. With the cut bottom end of the barrel facing up, measure carefully to find the widest point across the opening. Make a mark on the outside of the barrel at the center of this dimension as in Figure 1. Using a level or plumb bob, draw a straight line down the length of the barrel starting at the mark. Repeat for the opposite side of the barrel.

Making the Doghouse Front

When I originally designed these plans, I used a doghouse front panel that I purchased from J&J Dog Supplies, Inc. Using this premade part eliminated the need to cut a large hole out of plywood (a tedious task). Unfortunately, J&J no longer makes this part. The company has, however, provided a diagram that you can follow to make one.

1. Measure and cut the sheet of plywood as shown in Figure 2. There will be two scrap pieces. You can use the larger one (18" x 33") for another project, but the smaller one (12" x 33") is needed in step 1 of "Framing the Doghouse."

2. Measure and mark lines on the 30" x 30" piece of plywood as shown in Figure 3. You may be able to use the cut-off bottom of the barrel as a template for the circle. If that doesn't work, hammer a small nail into the plywood at the "X" in Figure 3. Tie one end of a 36" piece of string to the nail and the other end to a pencil. Wrap the string around the pencil until the diameter of the circle is just right (the string should be half as long as the diameter of the barrel). Use a small piece of duct tape to hold the string in place on the pencil. Draw the circle being careful not to rotate the pencil so that the string does not change in length.

3. Using a jig saw, cut along the dashed lines shown in the illustration. You will need to use a $1/2$" bit to drill pilot holes at the edge of the circle before cutting. Don't worry if your circle isn't absolutely perfect.

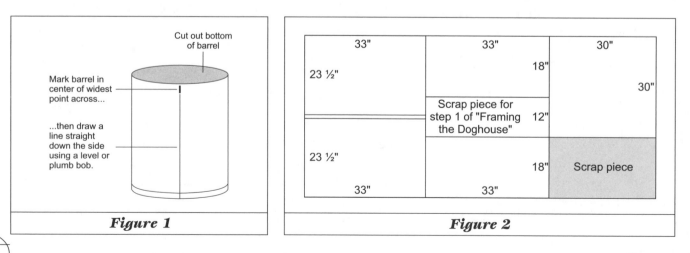

Figure 1

Figure 2

tunnels & accessories

Use the resulting cutout piece wherever the instructions call for the doghouse front.

Framing the Doghouse

1. Lay the doghouse front on top of the 12" x 33" piece of plywood so that the roof peak and one side are flush with the edge of the plywood. Using a carpenter's pencil, trace the outline of the pitched roof onto the plywood. Remove the doghouse front. Measure 7 $\frac{1}{4}$" from the roof peak and draw a line. Measure 12 $\frac{1}{2}$" from the center of the roof peak on each side so that the whole thing is 25" wide. Your lines should match Figure 4. Cut out the plywood along your marks. This piece will create the proper roof pitch for the rear of the tunnel frame so that it matches the front.

2. Cut four pieces for the roof supports from a 2x4 and four pieces from another 2x4 for the vertical corner supports of the doghouse. Each of these pieces must have a 20° angle cut on one end as shown in Figure 5. By cutting them in one step, you will have to make fewer cuts. Each cut produces two boards with an identical pitch (geometry in action). Set the angle on your circular saw to 20° and rest it on the wide side of the 2x4. When you cut this way, one edge of each piece will be longer than the other. The lengths of both edges are given in Figure 6. Four 2x4 pieces are cut so that the long edge is 16 $\frac{1}{4}$" and the short edge is 16". Four 2x4 pieces are cut so that the long edge is 24" and the short edge is 23 $\frac{1}{2}$". After you make the angled cuts, reset your saw to 90°, measure the long and short edge of each piece and make the necessary right-angled cuts.

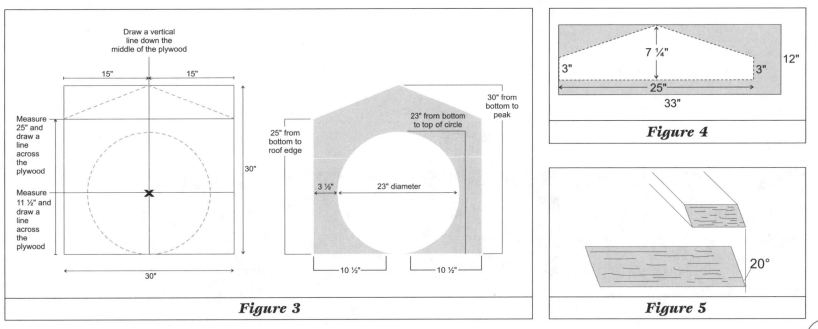

Figure 3

Figure 4

Figure 5

3. Fit together two of the shorter 2x4s as shown in Figure 7 to make a roof peak. Don't worry if the angle match is not exact. You can fill in the space with wood putty or caulk, and after painting, no one will know. Align the sides of the 2x4s with the top of the pitched roof of the doghouse front and clamp in place. Drill two pilot holes through the face of the doghouse front and into one of the 2x4s. Drive 2" drywall screws into the holes. Repeat for the other 2x4. Drill more pilot holes in each 2x4 (every 3"-4") and drive screws into them to securely attach the 2x4s.

4. Repeat step 3 to make a roof peak from 2x4s for the plywood template you made for the rear of the tunnel frame (see Figure 8).

5. Get the doghouse front assembly. Clamp one of the longer angled 2x4 pieces you cut in step 2 so that it forms one vertical corner support of the doghouse as shown in Figure 9. Make sure that it fits as snugly as possible next to the 2x4 of the roof peak. Drill pilot holes through the face of the doghouse front and into the 2x4 every 3"-4" as before. Drive in 2" long drywall screws. Repeat to attach another angled 2x4 to the other side of the doghouse front assembly.

NOTE: In all these steps, it helps to drill two pilot holes, drive two screws, release the clamps, drill more pilot holes, and drive the rest of the screws.

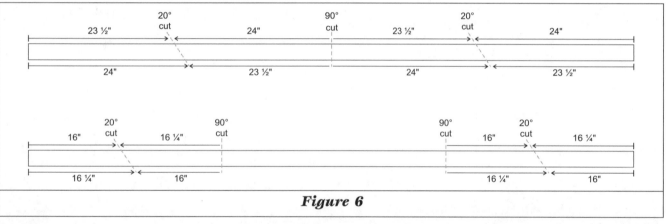

Figure 6

Figure 7

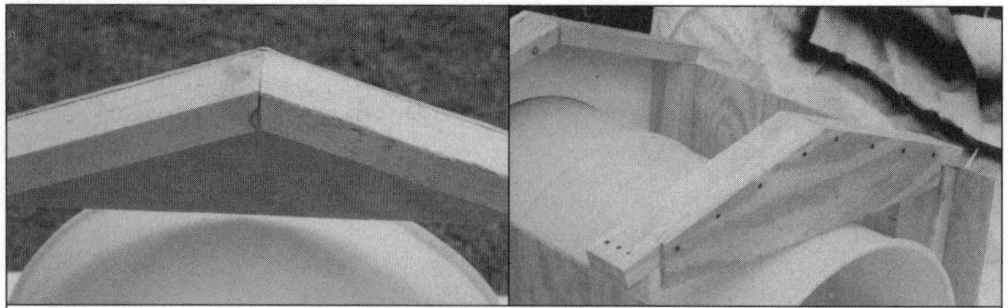

Figure 8

6. Drill two or three pilot holes straight down through the shorter, roof-support 2x4s into the tops of the longer, corner 2x4s. Drive 3" drywall screws into these holes.

7. Put together the back side assembly by attaching the two remaining angled 2x4 pieces to the roof peak 2x4s already attached to the plywood template. Drive in 3" drywall screws from the top to hold this assembly together as in Figure 10. Check your work frequently to ensure that the back assembly is a good match to the doghouse front assembly.

Mounting the Barrel

1. Cut the following pieces from the remaining 2x4 stud:

   2 – 30" long
   2 – 10" long

2. The two 30" pieces you cut will be side supports for the barrel. The lines you made on the barrel in step 4 of "Preparing the Barrel" will be the centerlines for positioning these 2x4 side supports. Draw several marks $1^{3}/_{4}$" on each side of these centerlines and connect

them so that you have two parallel lines $3^{1}/_{2}$" apart (with the original line in between). Position one of the 30" long 2x4s on the side of the barrel within the lines. Clamp the 2x4 in place and drill two $^{1}/_{4}$" holes through the 2x4 and the barrel. Make sure the holes are at least 12" apart. Attach the 2x4 to the barrel using the following sequence: feed a nylon bolt through from the inside of the barrel, then as it emerges through the hole in the 2x4, add a washer and nut. Tighten the nut with the wrench. Repeat this process to attach a side support to the other side of the barrel.

NOTE: Most barrels have ribs spaced about 12" apart. The wall of the barrel is thinner there, and I like to drill at this point. This also helps keep the head of the nylon bolt from catching a dog as it races through.

3. Make a note of which is the front end of the barrel (no lip) and which is the back (with the lip intact to help hold the fabric portion of the chute). Put the doghouse front on the barrel, making sure that everything lines up and the barrel is not twisted. Then, drill pilot holes and drive 3" drywall screws through the front 2x4 corner pieces into the ends of the 2x4 barrel supports. Repeat for the rear of the tunnel frame, using the back assembly you made.

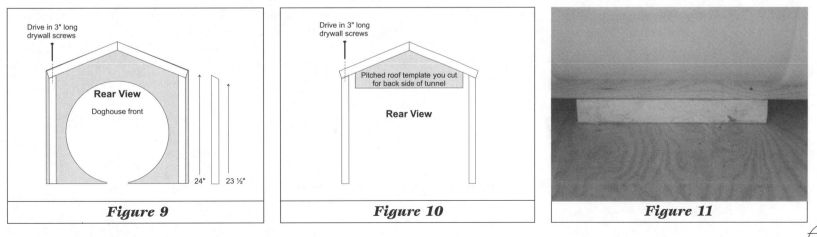

Figure 9

Figure 10

Figure 11

4. Take one of the 10" long pieces of 2x4 and attach it to one of the 2x4 barrel side supports, centering it between the two bolts inside of the barrel as shown in Figure 11. Drill pilot holes and use 2" drywall screws. Repeat for the opposite side of the barrel.

Attaching the Doghouse Sides and Roof

1. The 23 ½" x 33" plywood pieces you cut are the sides of the doghouse. Attach these to the 10" piece of 2x4 and the two corner 2x4s on each side, using 2" drywall screws. A picture of the tunnel after you attach the sides is shown in Figure 12.

2. The 18" x 33" plywood pieces you cut form the roof. Attach these to the 2x4 roof supports. If you line them up so that the mill-cut edges are touching each other, the roof will look nicer. The roof "eaves" should hang over the top, covering the nastier parts of your work.

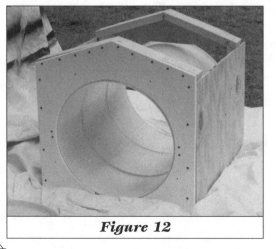

Figure 12

3. Measure the roof ridge flashing and cut to a length of 33" using a hacksaw or Dremel tool. Center the crease on the ridge of the roof (where the two pieces of plywood meet at the top of the roof) and tack down with 2" drywall screws, or shorter drywall screws if you have them.

Finishing the Tunnel

Paint or decorate the doghouse as you see fit. Plastic flowers from the craft store can be used to make window boxes sitting underneath painted windows if you are the Martha Stewart type. If you want to add handles, it makes the obstacle easier to carry.

A nonskid surface for the side of the barrel that will be the bottom of the tunnel opening is required. If you use exterior-rated adhesive caulk for this step, the job will last a long time.

1. Cut a piece of indoor-outdoor carpeting or a floor mat to a width of 24" and a length that is as long as your barrel.

2. Turn over the piece of carpeting or matting so that the backing (nonuseable) side faces you. With a caulk gun, spread a layer of adhesive exterior caulk over the entire surface. Use a putty knife or a scrap of wood to spread it evenly.

3. Carefully pick up the piece of carpeting so that the two edges almost touch and place it inside the bottom of the barrel, centering it between the two lines you previously made. Applying pressure, smooth down the carpeting so that it makes good contact with the inside surface of the barrel.

$f$abric chute for the closed tunnel

$t$he "Resource Guide" at the beginning of this book lists a number of sources for purchasing a commercially-made fabric chute. If you've decided to make your own chute instead, you can follow these plans. The finished chute is machine washable. The design for these plans was created by my wife, Rosemary Hoffman.

You can use ripstop nylon, which is available in a variety of colors at large fabric stores. However, ripstop nylon doesn't hold up well for outdoor use. It's so light that it blows in the slightest breeze and it isn't rugged enough for frequent use. If you're concerned about longevity, it's better to use packcloth or banner fabric, especially if you can find fabric with built-in UV protection to keep the material from deteriorating in the sun. I used 60" wide banner fabric from Hang-Em High Fabric which comes in a variety of bright colors. Seattle Fabrics carries other fabrics that will also work: coated nylon balloon cloth, 430 denier packcloth, and 200 denier 100 % nylon uncoated Solarmax Oxford. Seattle Fabrics also sells sample books for a nominal cost. Information for contacting these companies is included in the "Resource Guide" at the beginning of the book.

NOTE: USDAA requires the fabric to be less than 6 oz./sq. yd. or 420 denier, although the 430 denier fabric from Seattle Fabrics will probably pass the test unless someone sends it to a lab for analysis.

Materials Needed

- 8 ½ yards – ripstop nylon fabric, 50"-60" wide

  NOTE: If you want different colors for the top and bottom of the chute, get 4 ¼ yards of two different colors.

- 1 – large spool all-purpose thread

- 2 yards – 1" wide grosgrain ribbon (pronounced grow-grain)

- 1 – Large bungee cord to stretch around the barrel of your tunnel (get the longest one you can find)

  OR

- 1 – Belt with plastic, quick-release buckle

  NOTE: Cut this from a fanny pack, large dog collar, or backpack (see step 9). Alternatively, you can buy a buckle from Hang-Em High. It's part #JTB, 1" plastic black buckle. If you buy the buckle, however, you still need to get belt webbing.

Tools Needed

- Sewing machine
- Straight pins
- Marking chalk or pen
- Scissors or razor blade
- Tape measure

Directions

1. Measure the circumference of the tunnel barrel at the widest part the fabric tube will have to slip over. Add 6" to this measurement and divide by 2. Let's call this number "A". Divide A by 2 again, and write down that number; it's used in the pattern in Figure 1.

2. Lay out a little over 12' of the fabric (folded in half the way it comes off the bolt) on a smooth surface. Measure and mark the fabric as

shown in Figure 1. Pin the two layers together at intervals so they don't shift relative to each other and cut.

3. Unroll the rest of the fabric and use the cut piece as a pattern for cutting a second, identical piece. If you want to decorate your chute, it's easiest to do it now before the pieces are joined together.

4. Open the two pieces of fabric flat and lay one on the other with the "wrong" sides together. Pin the edges so that everything matches. Sew along the 12' long sides, making narrow seams less than $^1/_2$" wide.

5. Turn the fabric tube inside out and flatten the edges so that everything lays flat once again. Pin and sew a new seam, wider than the first, so that the raw fabric edges are contained. This is called a French seam.

6. Make a wide hem at the large end of the tube. Fold under about an inch of fabric, then fold a second time so that a 3" hem with no raw edges is formed. Pin and sew along the open edge of the hem.

7. Before proceeding, make sure the narrow end of the chute will slip over the tunnel barrel. If it doesn't fit, open one seam about 6" to form a V-shaped opening. Make sure this will fit.

8. Fold under 2" of the small open end, and then fold under another 2". Sew along the open edge. Pin grosgrain ribbon over this 2" hem and sew it to the chute to reinforce this edge.

9. You can either slide the fabric over the rigid tunnel and strap it in place with a bungee cord or you can make a buckle strap as shown in Figure 2. If you cut the buckle loose from an old fanny pack, dog collar, backpack, or something else, leave about 3"-4" of nylon webbing attached to the fixed end of the buckle and enough strap to tighten the snap on the adjustable end. You can always cut away the excess later. Sew the ends of the nylon webbing to the ribbon on the smaller end of the chute so that the webbing can be tightened to hold the chute onto the barrel.

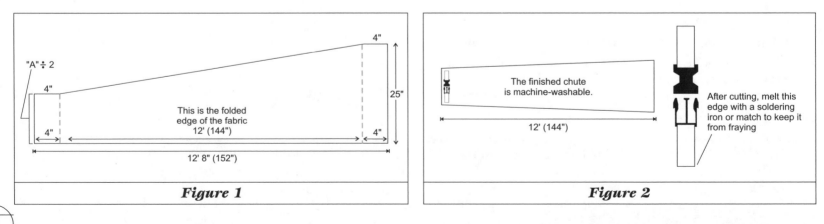

Figure 1

Figure 2

tunnels & accessories

pipe tunnel restraints

these plans are for pipe tunnel restraints that are easy to make and use. Three types of tunnel restraints are described, varying in weight, stability, and suitability for indoor or outdoor use.

Also included are some recommendations for ring stewards who need to mark exactly where tunnels should sit on courses at trials.

Concrete Tunnel Weights

These plans will make three *pairs* of weights.

Materials Needed

- 2 – 60 lb. bags Sakrete-brand concrete mix

  NOTE: This is cheap (about $4 a bag), but you may need help lifting the sacks.

- 6 – $5/16$" x 4" eyebolts
- 12 – $5/16$" fender washers
- 6 – $5/16$" toggle bolts
- 6 – 1 gallon disposable *plastic* paint buckets (the flimsier, the better for this job)
- 3 – bungee cords (longest available)
- 2 – 2" x 4" scrap pieces at least 4' long

Tools Needed

- Drill with $5/16$" bit or pliers and hot stove
- Wheelbarrow (optional)
- Shovel
- Garden trowel
- Water hose or bucket of water
- Gardening gloves or work gloves
- Utility knife

Directions

1. Find a place to work that's flat, but that you don't mind messing up. An out of the way dirt or grass area about 6' square is ideal.

2. Remove the nuts with spring-loaded wings from the toggle bolts and dispose of the bolts.

3. Place the two scrap 2x4s parallel to each other on the ground, about 4" or 5" apart.

4. Make a $5/16$" hole in the center of the bottom of each paint bucket. If the bucket is sturdy, you can drill a hole. If it's a flimsy bucket (better for this job), make a hole by holding one of the discarded toggle bolts by its head with pliers, putting it near a red-hot stove or flame, and then using it to melt a hole through the bottom of the bucket. Be careful *not* to set the bucket on fire and have a bucket of water nearby in case you do.

5. Prepare each bucket as follows: Thread a fender washer on an eyebolt, put the bolt through the hole in the bottom of the bucket, add another fender washer on the inside of the bucket, and top it off with the nut you removed from the toggle bolt as shown in Figure 1.

6. Rest the six bucket assemblies on the scrap 2x4s as shown in Figure 2.

7. Prepare the Sakrete. Be sure to wear gloves while working with it as the lime in the mix is corrosive to your skin. It's easiest to make a big batch of Sakrete in a wheelbarrow and then shovel it where you need it. Two bags of Sakrete will make about six gallons of concrete. Dump the two bags of Sakrete in the wheelbarrow bed—don't open the sacks yet. Then, take your shovel and with a quick snap, thrust it into the sack like you're killing a vampire. Make several cuts like this with your shovel and then lift the paper sack. It will tear and open, leaving the Sakrete in the wheelbarrow. Add a little water at a time, mixing it up with the shovel. Wait, and then add some more water. You want a consistency like mud pies or brownie batter.

   NOTE: Don't make the mix too wet; you can always add water but you can't take it away!

8. Shovel the Sakrete mix into the paint buckets resting on the 2x4s, using a big shovel or a garden trowel. Use a stick or the trowel to pack in the concrete, making sure there are no air pockets. Let it set for at least a day, longer if the weather is cool or damp. If it looks like rain, cover the buckets with a tarp.

9. When the concrete is set, turn the weight over so that the eyebolt is up. Use a utility knife to make several cuts in the bucket, and then peel away the plastic.

You now have six 20 lb. weights for holding pipe tunnels in place. To secure a tunnel, place a tunnel weight on either side of the opening and hook a bungee cord to each of the two eyebolts. Make sure the bungee is not so tight that it closes the tunnel mouth to smaller than regulation size.

Wooden Tunnel Holders

These plans will make two *pairs* of supports.

Materials Needed

- 1 – half-sheet (48" x 48") CDX plywood, preferably pressure-treated, $^1/_2$" thick
- 4 – pieces 2" x 4" x 8' framing lumber
- 1 – box #6 or #8 x 3" drywall screws
- 1 – box #6 or #8 x 1 $^1/_2$" or 1 $^5/_8$" drywall screws
  - 16 – $^1/_4$" eye screws
  - 4 – bungee cords, longest available

Tools Needed

- Drill with $^1/_{16}$" and $^3/_{16}$" bits
- Circular saw
- Electric screwdriver or Phillips-head bit for drill
- Spring-loaded carpenter's clamps
- Carpenter's ruler or tape measure
- Carpenter's pencil
- Flat-head screwdriver

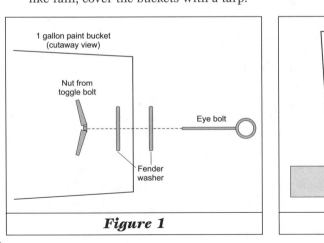

Figure 1

1 gallon paint bucket (cutaway view)

Nut from toggle bolt

Eye bolt

Fender washer

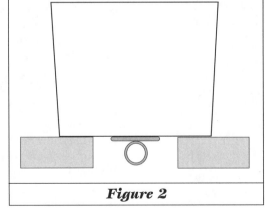

Figure 2

Directions

1. Have your lumberyard or home center cut the half-sheet of plywood for you, if possible. Otherwise, make cuts as shown in Figure 3.

2. Cut the 2x4s into 24 pieces, each 16" long.

3. Pipe tunnels vary slightly in diameter so it's best to custom-fit your tunnel if possible. Set the tunnel on one of the cut pieces of plywood as shown in Figure 4 (the long edge of the plywood is shown). Then, place two of the 16" long 2x4s on the plywood on each side of the tunnels as shown. Mark with a pencil where the 2x4s are resting on the plywood.

   NOTE: If you don't have a tunnel available, make a line down the center of the plywood piece (exactly 16" from each edge). Next, make a series of marks 6" on either side of this line. Connect these marks with a ruler or straight edge.

4. Clamp two 2x4s on each side of the plywood, using the marks you've made as guides and making sure they are exactly parallel. Turn the assembly over and drill pilot holes (using the $^1/_{16}$" bit) through the plywood and into the 2x4s. Drive six 1 $^1/_2$" drywall screws into each 2x4. Double check to make sure the tunnel rests comfortably in the cradle.

5. Add a third 16" long 2x4 to each stack as shown. Again, it's easiest if you have a tunnel handy so that you can make a custom fit. Mark the position of this 2x4 with a pencil, remove the tunnel, and clamp the 2x4s in place. Drill six pilot holes in each one, then drive 3" drywall screws through the top 2x4 and into the bottom one. Check

to make sure the tunnel rests in the cradle. If necessary, just unscrew the 2x4s and move things around.

6. Measure 4" from the end of each of the top 2x4s and make marks in the center of the 2x4 at these points. These marks will be 8" apart. Drill a $^3/_{16}$" pilot hole at each mark, then start an eye screw in each hole. To tighten the screws, stick the blade of a flat-head screwdriver through the hole in the eye screw and turn clockwise using the handle of the screwdriver for leverage.

7. Paint the tunnel base before using.

To secure a tunnel, hook a bungee cord to each of the two eye screws, stretch over the top of the tunnel, and hook on the corresponding eye screws on the other side of the base. Make sure the bungee cords are not so tight that they close the tunnel mouth to smaller than regulation size.

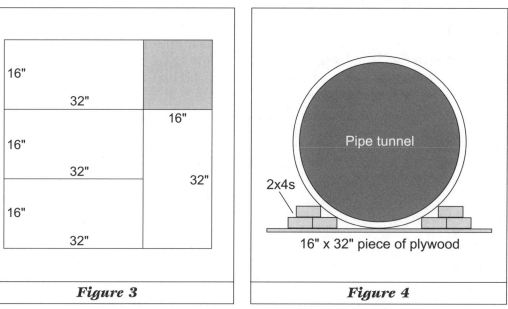

| Figure 3 | Figure 4 |

Figure 3

Figure 4

16"
32"
16"
32"
16"
32"
16"
32"

Pipe tunnel

2x4s

16" x 32" piece of plywood

Saddlebag Tunnel Holders

These are the easiest of the three tunnel support designs to make, but probably the least efficient. You will need a lot of them to weight a tunnel since each saddlebag only weighs 10 lbs.

These plans will make two pairs of saddlebags.

Materials Needed

- 4 – soft-sided PVC lunch coolers, approximately 4" x 5" x 8", with strap handle
- 1 – bag play sand
- 2 – bungee cords (longest available) or canvas belts

Tools Needed

- Garden trowel

Making the Saddlebags

1. Shovel sand into the zippered compartment of each soft-sided lunch cooler, and then close the zipper.

2. You can strap the coolers over the tunnel like saddlebags on a horse, connecting them with bungee cords. However, if you don't mind a little sewing, use a canvas belt about 5' long and sew both ends so that it makes a permanent set of saddlebags that can be draped over the tunnel to hold it in place.

Marking the Position of Tunnels on Course

If you are just training at a club site or in your backyard, you probably don't care exactly where the tunnel sits. If a fast or heavy dog whips through the tunnel and moves it, it's really no big deal. However, at a trial, it *is* a big deal.

Now that you have some ideas of different supports you can make to keep tunnels in place, let's look at how to know where the tunnel is supposed to be before you stake it down.

Materials Needed

All materials in this list are optional (see directions to determine what you need).

- 1 – roll duct tape
- 1 – piece tailor's chalk (available in fabric stores)
- 12 – bottles carpenter's chalk, preferably in bright colors such as red or orange (for grass fields) or blue or white (for dirt)
- Utility knife to open top of bottle
- 1 – bag golf tees
- 1 – roll surveyor's tape
- Scissors
- Sharp pencil or nail

If you are a ring steward who has to watch a tunnel, you know what a drag the highest height classes are. There you are, minding your own business and working on your tan, and those infernal black-and-white dogs come through to make a mockery of your tunnel placement.

If you are a judge or a ring steward who is responsible for one or more tunnels, you'll want to know where the tunnel belongs *before* you put restraints on it.

Before marking the position of tunnels as recommended below, make sure the judge is done with the final tweaking, and all the tunnels are exactly where they are supposed to be.

- If the trial is indoors on carpet or matting, you can make small strips of duct tape or use tailor's chalk to mark the position of the tunnel. Outline both openings of the tunnel. If the tunnel is set in a curve, it's not a bad idea to mark each of the curves at the apex or inflection point (the point where the tunnel changes from one direction to another).

- If the trial is outdoors or indoors on sod, my favorite trick is to buy several bottles of carpenter's chalk. Although you go through it fairly quickly, it's cheap. Figure on needing about two bottles for every course to be run. You want the kind that comes in a dispenser bottle with a plastic tip that looks like a catsup bottle in a diner. To erase the chalk lines, just scuff them with your feet.

- Another trick for marking obstacle position outdoors (not just tunnels, but broad jumps, the end of weave poles, or whatever) is to cut plastic surveyor's tape into 1" squares. Then, make a hole in the center of each with a sharp pencil or nail and push a golf tee through the hole you've made. These are especially nice for marking things outside.

hapter three

Contact Obstacles

Making Climbing Slats

I'll admit it—slats are giving me fits. The changing obstacle specifications from each of the major agility organizations have been a real headache. And, when you consider that all of these organizations have slightly different requirements, it gets worse.

Many people ask me if there is a single set of slats that will work for all agility organizations. Under the rules in effect at the time of this writing, the answer is "no"—at least not to the *exact* dimensions specified. The following are the current slat specifications for AKC, NADAC/ASCA, and USDAA at the time of this printing. This information is provided only as a reference for your convenience. It's a good idea to check the current rules if you're building a contact obstacle for competition. Most of the organizations have up-to-date copies of their rulebooks or equipment specifications on their websites.

Organization	Thickness	Width	Notes
AKC	$^3/_8$" to $^1/_2$"	$^3/_4$" to 1 $^1/_2$"	Slat edges should be rounded or beveled so they aren't sharp; a $^1/_4$" radius is recommended
NADAC	$^3/_8$" or less	$^3/_4$" to 1 $^1/_2$"	
USDAA—Upper third of A-frame	$^1/_2$" to $^3/_4$"	$^3/_4$" to 1 $^1/_2$"	Less than $^3/_4$" required; $^1/_2$" to $^3/_4$" are "strongly encouraged"
USDAA—Lower two-thirds of A-frame	$^1/_4$" to $^1/_2$"	$^3/_4$" to 1 $^1/_2$"	

Worse yet, it is nearly impossible to find lumber in these dimensions. Unless you live in a city with a lumberyard the size of ancient Persia, you really have to take potluck. I'm in a medium-sized city, so I'm restricted to finding what I can.

The kind of wood you need to make slats that meet these specifications won't be located in the regular lumber section of your local home center or lumberyard, but rather in a section called "Millwork." This is where chair rails, molding for door frames, and such is kept. I found two good possibilities in plain, rectangular millwork.

- One type is $^3/_8$" x $^3/_4$" with a slightly rounded edge. I put the rounded edge on the "downhill" side of each slat. This type of slat will be acceptable for A-frames used in AKC and NADAC. It will also be acceptable for two-thirds of a USDAA A-frame, but you would have to use something else for the slats on the top third of the A-frame.

- I also found some $^7/_{16}$" x 2" rectangular millwork. This needs to be *ripped* in half. Ripping is cutting wood with the grain, parallel to the long edge of the lumber. I hate ripping lumber. It's hard to do it right and often it just breaks. These slats would be $^1/_{16}$" too thin to meet USDAA recommendations for the top third of the A-frame, but I'm betting no one will get upset over the lost $^1/_{16}$". With a couple of coats of sand paint, the slats will be $^1/_2$" thick and acceptable to all of the organizations except NADAC.

Shop around and do the best you can. If you're just using your equipment for practice and not for trials, you don't need to be as precise.

NOTE: Some agility equipment manufacturers, such as MAX 200/Pipe Dreams, sell slat kits that contain everything you need. You may want to check around and compare the cost of a commercial product vs. hunting for lumber and preparing the slats yourself.

contact obstacles

Painting Contact Obstacles

See "Painting Wooden Obstacles" at the beginning of the book for information on selecting paint.

Materials Needed

- 1 – bag play sand

  OR

- 1 – container of Skid-Tex

  NOTE: Some other additives for creating a good, nonslip surface on the contacts are Skid-Free, No-Skid, and Deck-Tec.

- White primer paint

- Yellow paint for the contact zones

- A different color paint for the final coat on the rest of the obstacle

Tools Needed

- Disposable 4" or 6" mini-rollers

- Disposable paint trays

- Paintbrushes

- Carpenter's ruler or tape measure

- Pencil or marker

- (If using play sand) Kitchen strainer with window screen-like basket

Directions

1. Coat the top surface of the ramps with primer and let it dry.

   If you are using sand to create a nonslip surface: Coat the area between any two slats with primer. Sprinkle sand through the strainer onto the wet primer until you have a thin, solid layer covering the area.

Don't worry about excess sand—you'll brush off whatever doesn't stick later. Repeat for the next set of slats and section of wood until the whole top side of each ramp is coated with primer and sand.

If you are using Skid-Tex to create a nonslip surface: Just put a coat of primer across the entire top side of each ramp.

2. Turn each ramp over, apply a coat of primer to the underside, and let it dry. (If you used sand in step 1, brush off any sand that didn't stick as you're flipping each ramp over.)

Organization	A-Frame	Dogwalk	Seesaw
AKC	42"	42"	42"
NADAC	42"	36" to 42"	36" to 42"
USDAA	42"	36"	36"

3. Turn the ramps over again. Measuring from the bottom of each ramp, mark the top of each contact zone appropriately.

4. (Optional) If you are using Skid-Tex or another additive, mix it into your colored paint according to the directions on the package.

5. Cover each ramp with a coat of colored paint—yellow for the contact zones and whatever color you chose for the rest of each ramp.

6. Apply a second coat of paint if needed.

Plans Included

In this section, you will find the following plans:

- Welded Aluminum or Steel A-Frame

- Wooden A-Frame

- Rejuvenating and Refurbishing an A-Frame

- Welded Aluminum or Steel Dogwalk

- Adjustable Seesaw

- Contact Training Hoops

Welded aluminum or steel a-frame

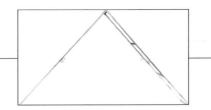

the best A-frame skeletons are made from steel or aluminum, but most do-it-yourself builders don't have the equipment or the expertise for welding. Aluminum welding, in particular, is extremely difficult and is a job for professionals only.

NOTE: The term *skeleton* is used to describe the frame or supporting structure of an A-frame to which you attach a plywood surface.

I've bought A-frame skeletons from commercial equipment vendors, but the problem is the shipping cost. A-frames are too large to be shipped by UPS, so they have to go motor freight. Any of you who have dealt with motor freight companies know that 1) it's devilishly expensive; and 2) they aren't oriented toward the consumer market. If you are having a bulldozer trucked to Kalamazoo, they are happy to work with you; however, if you want to get an A-frame from either the Right Coast or Left Coast to an agility "black hole" (Scot Bartley's term) in the middle somewhere, you can pay from $150-$200 in shipping. And it will get there when the motor freight company is darn good and ready.

Your best bet is to have the A-frame skeleton welded locally. These plans describe the steps involved in getting this done and include professionally-drawn blueprints. Just choose the material you want to use—aluminum or steel—and then take the appropriate set of plans to a welder.

Choosing the Materials

You have two choices of materials for an A-frame skeleton: steel or aluminum. Following is a summary of their advantages and disadvantages.

	Aluminum	Steel
Weight	Light	Heavy
Cost	Expensive	Cheap
Finding a welder	Difficult	Easy
Weather-resistance	Excellent	Very poor

An aluminum skeleton made from these plans will weigh 30 lbs. A steel skeleton will weigh 50 lbs. Once the plywood is added, the completed aluminum A-frame will be 120 lbs. and the steel one will be 150 lbs.

I wanted a lightweight A-frame that would hold up well in the Mississippi climate: wet and cold in the winter, wet and hot in the summer. Steel rots. Aluminum does not, especially if you pay extra to have it anodized. I chose aluminum.

Finding a Welding Shop

Let your fingers do the walking. I found a local machine shop in the Yellow Pages. The first place I picked out had an advertisement that said, "Quick and reliable machine work, welding and repairs. Commercial—Industrial—Individual. Family Owned since 1964." The "individual" part caught my eye since I didn't want to be treated like some idiot. Better yet, the place was not too far from my house.

I drove over and met the proprietor, Alan Patrick. Alan gave me a look when I whipped out the blueprints since he had never seen dog agility, and he spends a lot more time welding trailers than A-frames. However, he was a good sport about it, and we negotiated a price that seemed about right to me. He said it would take him about a week; most of that time involved waiting for the raw materials to be ordered and shipped to him. True to his word, he was done when he said he would be.

The cost of the welding (including materials) for the A-frame in aluminum was $430 plus tax. That may sound like a lot, but the cost of the

contact obstacles

raw materials is high. Depending on the cost of labor in your area, I would guess you should expect to pay about $500 to have the A-frame welded locally (budget another $100 for wood, paint, and hardware).

Special Notes for the Welder

It is very important that the pipe which forms the hinge of the A-frame is welded to the corner of the square tubing and not centered on the square tubing (see "enlarged view of hinge tubing" on the plans.) If the round pipe is centered on the square pipe, the A-frame will not be able to fully open. Please point this out to the welder you select.

If you have a steel A-frame made, another option is to ask the welder to replace the pipe with a continuous hinge. A suitable hinge is available from McMaster-Carr. The hinge specifications are: 0.090" thick, 3" wide, 36" long, 0.25" pin diameter, 1" knuckle length (part # 15665A429). If you choose this option, you still want to remove the pin and replace it with a smaller one as described later on.

Making the A-Frame More Portable

If you desire, there are several ways that you can make the aluminum or steel A-frame in these plans more portable:

- Make a removable hinge pin so that the skeleton can be broken down into two pieces.

    The plans call for the A-frame to have a permanent rod connecting the two sides so that you can fold up the A-frame to move or store it. However, the aluminum skeleton with wood attached is 120 lbs. and may be too much for one person to move. If you replace the rod with a removable pin, you will be able to detach the two pieces to move the A-frame. Each piece will weigh 60 lbs. which can more likely be carried by one individual. I removed the $^3/_8$" diameter steel rod specified in the plans and replaced it with a $^5/_{16}$" aluminum rod. This process is described in the next section.

- Use thinner plywood to cover the skeleton.

    If your A-frame is to be used by big dogs or by all sizes of dogs, you need to use $^1/_2$" plywood. However, if you have only small dogs and you want to reduce the weight of the obstacle, you can use $^3/_8$" or even $^1/_4$" plywood. An aluminum A-frame with $^1/_4$" plywood attached will weigh about 75 lbs. So, if you make the A-frame so that you can divide it into two pieces, as described above, it will weigh less than 40 lbs. per piece. It won't support a dog that weighs over 20 lbs. though. Attaching the plywood is discussed in "Attaching the Plywood 'Skin'" later on.

(Optional) Making a Removable Pin

Machinists like things to have very tight tolerances. The A-frame that Alan Patrick made for me was no exception. The steel rod he used as a hinge pin on the A-frame was really difficult to remove.

Materials Needed

- 1 – $^5/_{16}$" diameter metal rod, 3' long

    NOTE: Small Parts, Inc. has these. For an aluminum A-frame, order item W-ZRA-5-36. For a steel A-frame, order item W-ZRXX-5-36.

- WD-40 or similar penetrating oil

Tools Needed

- Allen wrench or hex driver attachment for reversible electric drill or screwdriver
- Screwdriver (with the longest shaft you can find in your workshop)
- Hammer
- Set of sawhorses or some cinderblocks

contact obstacles

Directions

1. Lay the A-frame skeleton so that it's flat on the sawhorses or cinderblocks.

2. With an assistant holding the A-frame steady, use the screwdriver and hammer to start pounding out the steel rod . Once you get the rod out as far as you can, apply WD-40 to the end of it. Pound the rod back the other way. This will help grease the rod and make it easier to remove in the long run. Once you reach the handle of the screwdriver going back the other way, insert the $^5/_{16}$" replacement pin. Hammer on the end of the new pin to pound out the rest of the old rod.

3. Center the $^5/_{16}$" pin in the hinge and stand up the A-frame skeleton to test it.

Attaching the Plywood "Skin"

I use $^1/_2$" plywood. If the A-frame is to be used exclusively by smaller dogs, however, you can use thinner plywood as described in "Making the A-Frame More Portable." If you live near a seacoast, you can get marine-grade plywood. It's expensive, but will last a long time. If you are inland, like me, you will have to use exterior-grade plywood, which has an "X" after the grade—A, B, C, or D. The grade indicates the smoothness of the surface. AB plywood has one very smooth surface and one pretty good surface. CD plywood has one not-so-great surface and one lousy surface. Since the C-side will be covered with paint and slats, and no one will see or use the D-side, CDX plywood works fine and is cheaper.

Materials Needed

- 3 – 4' x 8' sheets $^1/_2$" plywood, CDX or marine grade

  NOTE: If the home center or lumberyard will cut the plywood free of charge, have them cut two sheets to 66" x 36" and cut the third sheet into two 42" x 36" pieces.

- 50 – $^1/_4$" x 2" carriage bolts

  NOTE: Substitute $^1/_4$" x 1 $^1/_2$" carriage bolts if using $^1/_4$" plywood.

- 50 – $^1/_4$" nuts and lock washers to fit bolts

  OR

  50 – lock nuts with nylon inserts

Tools Needed

- Drill with $^1/_8$" and $^1/_4$" bits
- Circular saw, if cutting the plywood yourself
- Socket wrench or nut driver to fit $^1/_4$" nuts
- Hammer
- Carpenter's ruler
- Measuring tape
- Pencil or marker
- Spring-loaded clamps or C-clamps
- Set of sawhorses or some cinderblocks

Directions

1. If you had the plywood cut for you, proceed to step 2. If not, use a circular saw to cut two of the plywood sheets to 66" x 36". Cut the third sheet into two 42" x 36" pieces.

2. Lay the A-frame so that it's flat and well supported on the sawhorses or cinderblocks. If you previously detached the two pieces of the A-frame to make a removable pin, it will make working on the skeleton easier as you can lay out just one piece at a time.

3. Line up a piece of 42" x 36" plywood on the *bottom* edge (farthest from the hinge) of the skeleton. (If the two pieces of your A-frame are attached, work on one and then the other.) It's best if one of the original edges of the plywood is on the side nearest the hinge. The

lower-grade (rougher) side of the plywood should be next to the skeleton while the higher-grade (smoother) side should be facing up. Once the plywood is lined up, clamp it to the skeleton.

4. Next, make guide lines for drilling the holes to mount the plywood. You want the holes centered in the aluminum or steel tubing, which is 1" across. First measure 36" from the bottom edge of the skeleton and mark a line across the plywood at this point. This is the center of crosspiece tubing beneath the wood. Next, make a series of marks that are $1/2$" from the left, right, and bottom edges of the plywood. Connect these marks with a carpenter's ruler.

5. Drill $1/8$" pilot holes at about 18" intervals along your guide lines. Then re-drill the holes using the $1/4$" bit. It is necessary to do it in two steps in order to get through the steel or aluminum tubing.

6. Insert carriage bolts into the holes you made, using the hammer to help them along if necessary. Place a lock washer on the end of each bolt, then finger-tighten a nut on each one to hold the washer in place. (If you use nylon locknuts, you will have to use a wrench to start the nuts.) Remove the clamps after all of the nuts are in place. Tighten each nut using the nut driver or socket wrench

7. Clamp a 66" x 36" piece of plywood to the skeleton, making sure the seams where the two plywood pieces meet are as close as possible. Again, place the original edge of the plywood at the seam rather than an edge where you cut. Repeat steps 4 through 6, but in step 4, measure 36" from the *top* of the A-frame skeleton (where the hinge is).

8. Repeat steps 2 through 7 for the other half of the A-frame skeleton.

Attaching the Chains

This A-frame is sturdy enough to lower all the way to the ground for training. To do so, you will need 9' of chain for each side. If you are only going to use the obstacle at full height, you need 6-7' of chain for each side. If you're not sure, buy 9' for each side and let the excess hang.

Materials Needed

- 2 – 7' or 9' lengths of chain with $3/16$" links
- 2 – $3/16$" galvanized breakable links
  NOTE: These are also called quick links or repair links.
- 2 – $5/16$" spring snaps
- (Optional) Red nail polish or plastic tape

Tools Needed

- Carpenter's ruler or tape measure

Instructions

1. With an assistant, set the A-frame so that the apex is at the highest point you will need. It should be 5'6" for AKC, NADAC, USDAA Performance, and USDAA 12" Championship division or 6'3" for all other USDAA Championship divisions.

2. Use a breakable link to attach one end of a chain to one of the D-rings that are welded to the A-frame skeleton. Use the spring snap to attach one of the links on the other end of that chain to the D-ring on the opposite side of the skeleton. There should be a slight amount of slack in the chain. Repeat to assemble the other length of chain.

    NOTE: *Do not go under the A-frame right now—it's not safe until the chains are secure.*

4. With your assistant, spread the sides of the A-frame so that the chain is now taut. Measure the height at the apex. If it isn't correct, lift the A-frame, press the sides together slightly, and reattach the spring snap to a different link in the chain. Once you find the right link of the chain to set the height properly, mark it with a liberal amount of red nail polish, a piece of duct tape, or a nylon tie.

contact obstacles

Attaching Slats and Painting

Before you go shopping for the materials listed below, please read "Making Climbing Slats" on page 97.

Materials Needed

- 48 – linear feet of millwork

  NOTE: It's a good idea to buy some extra in case of accidents.

- 1 – box staples or brads that are about $^3/_8$" longer than the thickness of the slats

- (Optional) Carpenter's glue

Tools Needed

- Backsaw or mitre saw

- C-clamps or pistol-grip adjustable clamps with at least a 3" span

- Staple gun or electric nail gun that takes selected staples or brads

- Carpenter's ruler or tape measure

- Pencil or marker

- (Optional) Circular saw, jigsaw, or hand saw with the finest-toothed blade you can get

Mounting the New Slats

1. Cut the millwork into strips using the mitre saw or backsaw. If you try to use an electric saw, the millwork will splinter and make a mess. It needs to be cut by hand.

   NOTE: Rather than cutting the strips to the width of the A-frame, I cut them 1" longer than required (37" in this case). After mounting the strips, I use a circular saw to cut them flush to the A-frame edge.

2. Take apart your A-frame and put one of the side walls on sawhorses or on a flat surface where you can work easily. Position the slats on the top surface of the side wall so that the centers of the slats are spaced at 12" intervals with no slat falling within 4" of the top of the contact zone or the end of the frame. For each slat, be sure to take a measurement on both edges of the A-frame wall so that you're sure the slats are straight. As you work, use a pencil to mark the position of each slat.

3. Either have an assistant hold a slat in place or clamp the slat to the plywood using C-clamps, spring clamps, or pistol-grip adjustable clamps. Mount the strips to the plywood wall of the A-frame using staples or brads (screws will split the delicate millwork), securing it every 3"-4". Repeat until you have mounted all of the slats on each side of the A-frame. If you don't have an assistant, you can just keep moving the clamps to the next slat.

   NOTE: If you cut the slats long, as suggested in step 1, make the left edge flush with the left side of the A-frame and let the right edge hang over the other side of the A-frame. (Unless you are left-handed, in which case, reverse this.) If you want, you can place a thin layer of carpenter's glue on each slat before nailing or stapling it. However, if someone comes along and changes slat specifications next week, you'll be sorry you did this since the slats will be almost impossible to remove.

4. If you cut the slats long and let the ends of them hang over the edge of the A-frame, now is the time to trim them flush with the side of the A-frame using a circular saw, jigsaw, or hand saw with a very fine-toothed blade. The slats will *not* split if you use an electric saw here because they are supported by the plywood and cannot flex.

5. Paint the A-frame according to the instructions on page 98.

contact obstacles

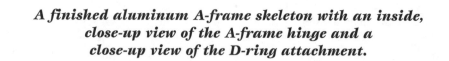

*A finished aluminum A-frame skeleton with an inside,
close-up view of the A-frame hinge and a
close-up view of the D-ring attachment.*

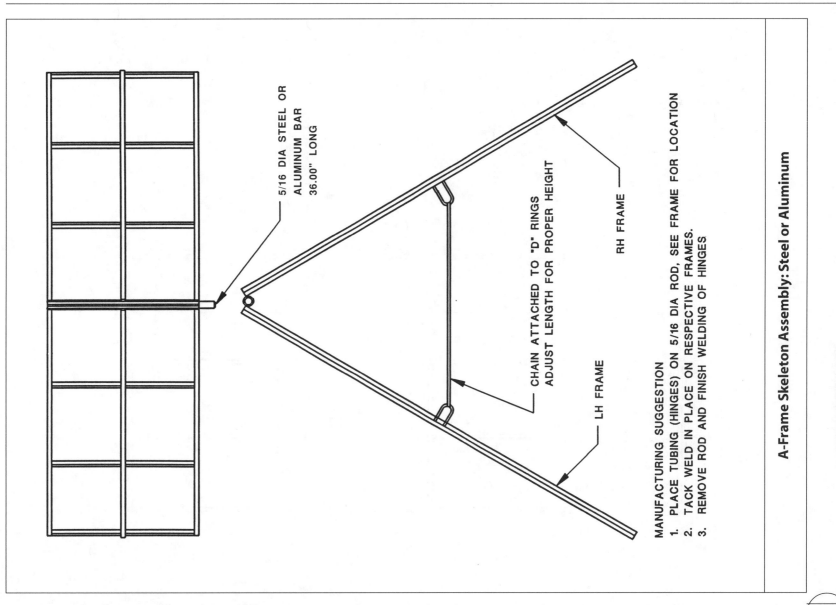

5/16 DIA STEEL OR
ALUMINUM BAR
36.00" LONG

CHAIN ATTACHED TO "D" RINGS
ADJUST LENGTH FOR PROPER HEIGHT

RH FRAME

LH FRAME

MANUFACTURING SUGGESTION
1. PLACE TUBING (HINGES) ON 5/16 DIA ROD, SEE FRAME FOR LOCATION
2. TACK WELD IN PLACE ON RESPECTIVE FRAMES.
3. REMOVE ROD AND FINISH WELDING OF HINGES

A-Frame Skeleton Assembly: Steel or Aluminum

ENLARGED VIEW OF
HINGE TUBING

.500 OD X .035 WALL
STEEL TUBING
9.00" LONG 2 REQD
TACK WELD IN PLACE
ALIGN 2 TUBES WITH
.375 DIA ROD
ALIGN CENTER OF TUBE
WITH TOP RAIL

"D" SHAPED 1/4" DIA
STEEL ROD
TACK WELDED AT
MIDPOINT

1" X 1" 1/16 WALL SQUARE
STEEL TUBING

108.00

9.00
REF

9.00

36.00 REF

34.00

16.50

35.50

35.50

Steel A-Frame

9.00 REF

9.00

36.00 REF

34.00

16.50

35.50

35.50

108.00

ENLARGED VIEW OF
HINGE TUBING

.500 OD X .035 WALL
STEEL TUBING
9.00" LONG 2 REQD
TACK WELD IN PLACE
ALIGN 2 TUBES WITH
.375 DIA ROD
WITH OTHER SIDE IN
LINE
ALIGN CENTER OF TUBE
WITH TOP OF RAIL

"D" SHAPED 1/4" DIA
STEEL ROD
TACK WELDED AT MIDPOINT

1" X 1" 1/16 WALL SQ
STEEL TUBING

Steel A-Frame

contact obstacles

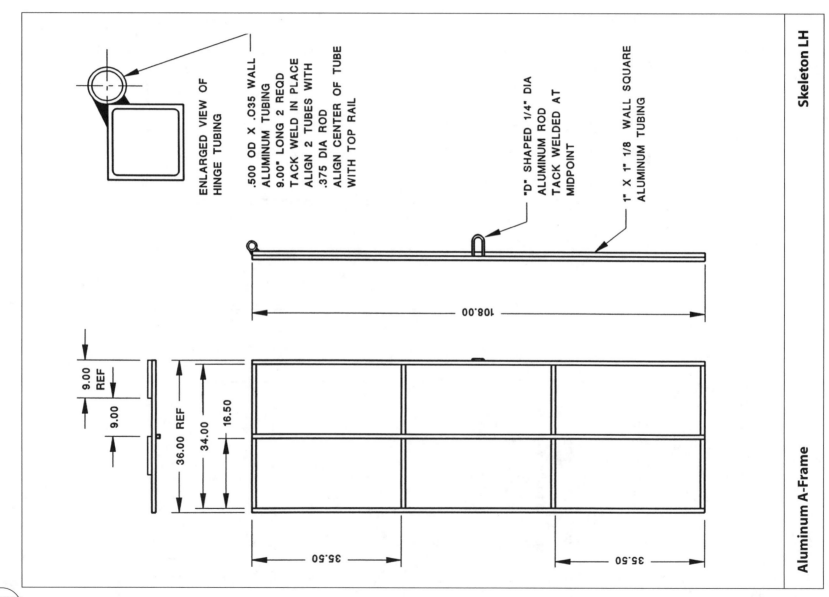

ENLARGED VIEW OF
HINGE TUBING

.500 OD X .035 WALL
ALUMINUM TUBING
9.00" LONG 2 REQD
TACK WELD IN PLACE
ALIGN 2 TUBES WITH
.375 DIA ROD
ALIGN CENTER OF TUBE
WITH TOP RAIL

"D" SHAPED 1/4" DIA
ALUMINUM ROD
TACK WELDED AT
MIDPOINT

1" X 1" 1/8 WALL SQUARE
ALUMINUM TUBING

108.00

9.00
REF

9.00

36.00 REF

34.00

16.50

35.50

35.50

contact obstacles

108

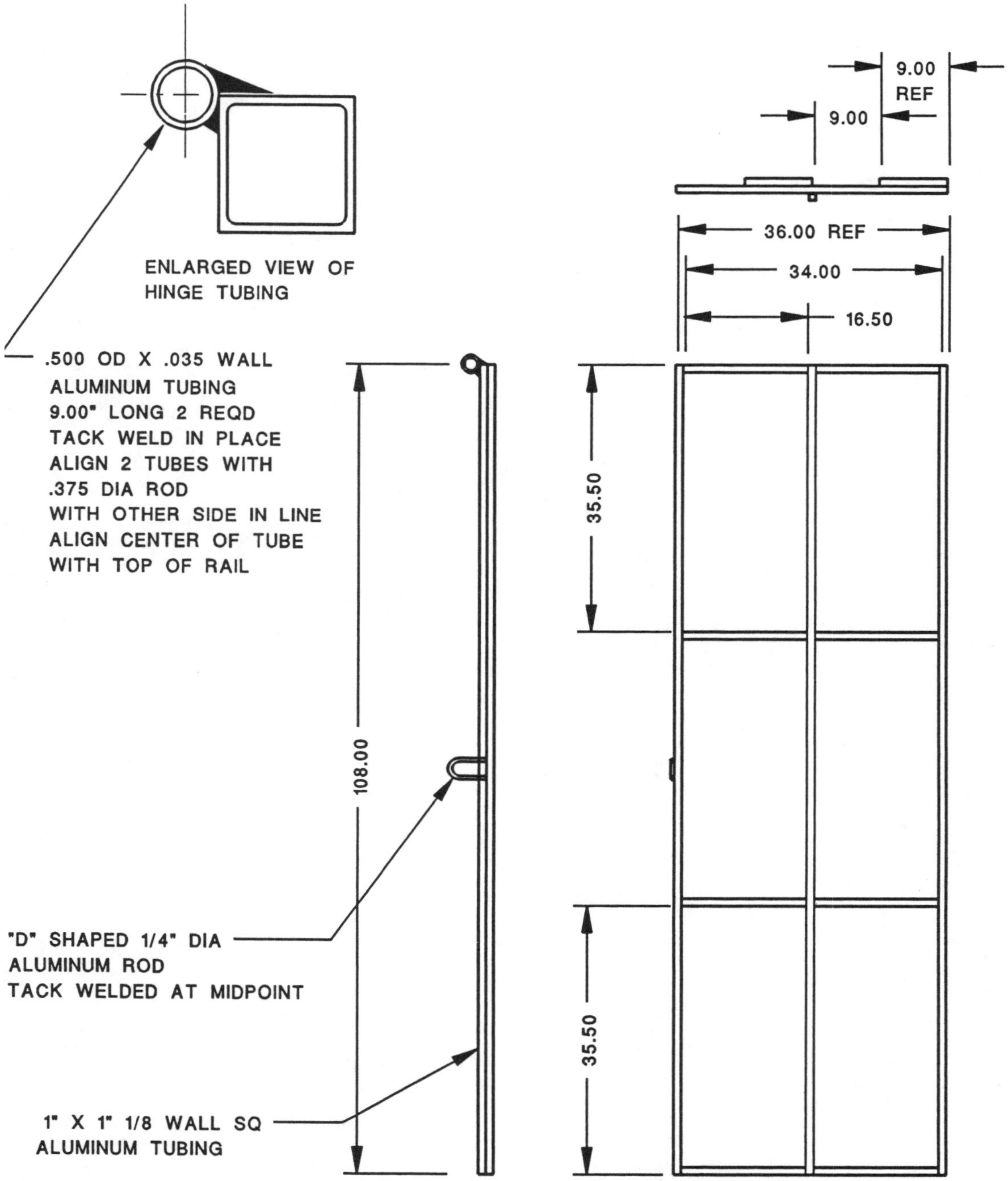

9.00 REF

9.00

36.00 REF

34.00

16.50

35.50

35.50

108.00

ENLARGED VIEW OF
HINGE TUBING

.500 OD X .035 WALL
ALUMINUM TUBING
9.00" LONG 2 REQD
TACK WELD IN PLACE
ALIGN 2 TUBES WITH
.375 DIA ROD
WITH OTHER SIDE IN LINE
ALIGN CENTER OF TUBE
WITH TOP OF RAIL

"D" SHAPED 1/4" DIA
ALUMINUM ROD
TACK WELDED AT MIDPOINT

1" X 1" 1/8 WALL SQ
ALUMINUM TUBING

Skeleton RH

Aluminum A-Frame

*W*ooden a-frame

One of the first obstacles I made was a wooden A-frame. It is heavy and hard to move around, and since I now have an aluminum A-frame, the wooden one has found a place in the backyard folded up and propped against a tree. However, if you do not want to spend the money for a welded skeleton and you aren't concerned with moving the A-frame around a lot, building a wooden A-frame is a viable alternative.

Materials Needed

- 3 – 4' x 8' sheets $^1/_2$" plywood, CDX or marine grade
- 1 – 4' x 4' half sheet $^1/_2$" plywood, CDX or marine grade
- 4 – 2" x 4" x 10' or 12' framing lumber (studs)

  NOTE: You need two additional studs if you make the optional supports in step 5 of "Building the Side Walls."
- 2 – 2" x 4" x 8' framing lumber (studs)
- 1 – 10' length 1 $^1/_2$" schedule 40 PVC
- 1 – $^1/_4$" diameter *unthreaded* steel rod at least 3' long
- 2 – 8' lengths of chain with 1 $^1/_4$" x $^3/_4$" links
- 4 – $^1/_4$" x 3" eyebolts
- 4 – $^1/_4$" nuts
- 4 – $^1/_4$" fender washers
- 4 – breakable links to match chain, approximately 2" x 1" (these are sometimes called quick links or repair links)
- 16 – #6 or #8 x 3" Phillips-head wood screws
- 16 – washers for wood screws (nylon preferred if available)
- 1 – 36" continuous hinge, part #15665A429 from McMaster-Carr

  NOTE: The hinge is designed for welding so you will need to drill screw holes for mounting it yourself.

- 1 – box #6 x 1 $^1/_2$" wood screws, pan head or round head
- 1 – box 1 $^1/_2$" or 1 $^5/_8$" exterior, fine-thread drywall screws
- 1 – box #6 x 2" galvanized exterior drywall screws

Before you go shopping for the materials listed below, please read "Making Climbing Slats" on page 97.

- 48 – linear feet of millwork

  NOTE: It's a good idea to buy some extra in case of accidents.
- 1 – box staples or brads that are about $^3/_8$" longer than the thickness of the slats

Tools Needed

- Circular saw
- Mitre saw or backsaw with the finest-toothed blade you can get
- Hacksaw or Dremel tool
- Drill with $^1/_8$", $^3/_{16}$", and $^1/_4$" bits
- Power screwdriver or drill bit for Phillips-head screws
- C-clamps or pistol-grip adjustable clamps with at least a 3" span
- Socket wrench or wrench to fit $^1/_4$" nuts
- Staple gun or electric nail gun that takes selected staples or brads
- Bench vise

- Hammer
- Pliers
- Carpenter's ruler or tape measure
- Pencil or marker
- (Optional) Carpenter's glue

Cutting the Lumber

1. Cut the 4' x 8' sheets of plywood into the following pieces:

   2 – 36" x 66" (each cut from one sheet)
   2 – 36" x 42" (cut from the third sheet)

2. Cut the millwork for the climbing slats into strips using the mitre saw or backsaw. If you use an electric saw, the millwork will splinter and make a mess. It needs to be cut by hand.

   NOTE: Rather than cutting the strips to the width of the A-frame, I cut them 1" longer than required (37" in this case). After mounting the strips, I use a circular saw to cut them flush to the A-frame edge.

3. Cut each of the four 2" x 4" x 10' or 12' studs to 108" (which is 9').

4. Cut three 29" long pieces from each of the two 2" x 4" x 8' studs (for a total of six 29" long pieces).

Building the Side Walls

1. Place two 108" 2x4s and three 29" 2x4s on a flat surface in the pattern shown in Figure 1. The boards should be resting on their wide side (the one measuring 3 $^1/_2$").

2. Lay a 36" x 42" piece of plywood and a 36" x 66" on top of this framework as shown in Figure 2. The dashed lines indicate the hidden 2x4s on the other side of the plywood.

3. Make sure all of the 2x4s are still correctly aligned and have not shifted. Drive 1 $^1/_2$ or 1 $^5/_8$" long drywall screws through the plywood and into the 2x4s. Place one screw about every 6".

4. Repeat steps 1 through 3 to build the other side wall for the A-frame.

5. (Optional) The A-frame will be stronger, but heavier, if you add diagonal support pieces to each side wall. If you wish to do this, you will need two additional 2" x 4" x 10' or 12' studs as mentioned in the materials list. Cut *two* of each of the supports shown in Figure 3. Once you have cut the supports as shown, place them under the plywood with the rest of the 2x4 framework as shown in Figure 4. Drive 1 $^1/_2$ or 1 $^5/_8$" long drywall screws through the plywood and into the 2x4s to secure. Place one screw about every 6".

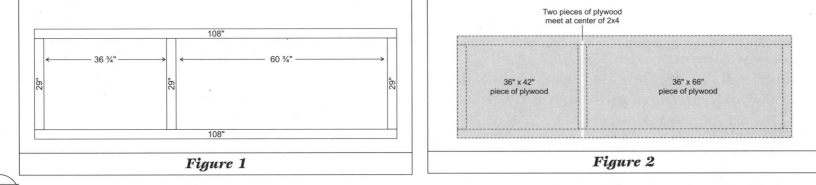

| 108" |
| 36 ¾" | 60 ¾" |
| 29" | 29" | 29" |
| 108" |

Figure 1

Two pieces of plywood meet at center of 2x4

36" x 42" piece of plywood   36" x 66" piece of plywood

Figure 2

contact obstacles

Mounting the Slats

1. Put one of the side walls on sawhorses or on a flat surface where you can work easily and have access to both sides at once. Position the slats on the top surface of the side wall so that the centers of the slats are spaced at 12" intervals with no slat falling within 4" of the top of the contact zone or the end of the frame. For each slat, be sure to take a measurement on both edges of the A-frame wall so that you're sure the slats are straight. As you work, use a pencil to mark the position of each slat.

2. Either have an assistant hold a slat in place or clamp the slat to the plywood using C-clamps, spring clamps, or pistol-grip adjustable clamps. Mount the strips to the plywood wall of the A-frame using staples or brads (screws will split the delicate millwork), securing it every 3"-4". Repeat until you have mounted all of the slats on each side of the A-frame. If you don't have an assistant, you can just keep moving the clamps to the next slat.

    NOTE: If you cut the slats long as suggested, make the left edge flush with the left side of the A-frame and let the right edge hang over the other side of the A-frame. (Unless you are left-handed, in which case, reverse this.) If you want, you can place a thin layer of carpenter's glue on each slat before nailing or stapling it. However, if someone comes along and changes slat specifications next week, you'll be sorry you did this since the slats will be almost impossible to remove.

3. If you cut the slats long and let the ends of them hang over the edge of the A-frame, now is the time to trim them flush with the side of the A-frame using a circular saw, jigsaw, or hand saw with a very fine-toothed blade. The slats will *not* split if you use an electric saw here because they are supported by the plywood and cannot flex.

Mounting the Hinge

1. Place the hinge on top of a scrap piece of wood on a sturdy, level surface. Clamp the the hinge in place and drill holes at 4"-6" intervals in both sides of the hinge. You want the holes to be bigger than the shaft of the mounting screws, but not so big that the screw heads can slip through. Start with the smallest drill bits and work up to the larger ones—no one can drill a $1/4$" hole in thick steel without drilling a smaller hole first. The drill will just bind up.

    NOTE: After you drill several holes, you can use these to temporarily mount the hinge to your piece of scrap wood. This will make it easier to drill the remaining holes.

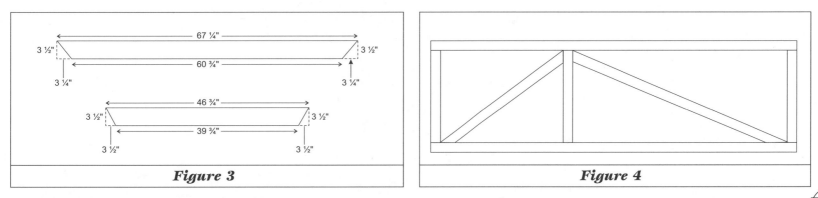

Figure 3   **Figure 4**

contact obstacles

2. Cut the steel rod to 38". A Dremel tool is handy for this task (wear goggles), but a hacksaw will work as well.

3. Make a mark 2" from the end of the rod, then clamp the rod in a bench vise so that the mark is just visible at the edge of the jaws. Using your bare hands or a pair of pliers, bend the rod so that it makes an "L" shape with 2" of rod forming the short leg of the "L" and 36" forming the long leg.

4. Set the A-frame on a flat, level surface with the two sides forming an angle to each other—it should be in the same position as when it's used, but just on its side.

5. Line up the hinge so that it is correctly positioned (see Figure 5) and drill $1/8$" pilot holes in four places. Drive in four wood screws and then check to make sure everything is lined up right before continuing. If you made a mistake, you only have to remove four screws instead of a dozen or more. If everything is right, then drill pilot holes for the remaining screws and drive the screws in place.

6. Rest the A-frame flat on the ground. Using a hammer and a nail, drive the hinge pin out of the hinge. Replace the hinge pin with the bent $1/4$" steel rod. In use, you should point the "handle" part of the rod toward the ground so that it does not present a potential hazard.

Attaching the Chains

1. With the A-frame still assembled, make a mark that is 57 $1/2$" from the top (where the hinges are) and 1 $3/4$" from the side. This mark should be centered side-to-side on one of the long 2x4s. Make three more marks for each long 2x4. These are where the eyebolts that hold the A-frame chains will be mounted.

2. Drill a $1/4$" hole through one of the marks.

3. Insert an eyebolt in the hole with the eye next to the 2x4. Check to see if any threads are protruding through the plywood. If not, remove the eyebolt and use the drill or a Dremel tool to enlarge the hole on the 2x4 side. You want just enough thread protruding through the plywood to get a good "bite," but not more than $1/8$" to $1/4$".

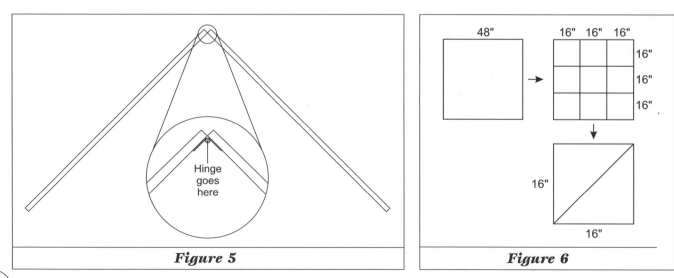

Figure 5

Hinge goes here

Figure 6

contact obstacles

4. Put a fender washer on the end of the eyebolt and mount the nut. If the nut will not "bite," remove the fender washer, tighten the nut a bit with the socket wrench, then remove the nut and replace the washer. Tighten the nut completely; there should be very little of the bolt protruding through the plywood.

NOTE: The end of the bolt will be right above a slat so that a dog's feet won't contact it. However, if you are concerned about it, either use a Dremel tool to remove any protruding thread, or cover the nut with a glob of silicone caulk. Make sure it's tight before you mess with it because you might not be able to tighten or loosen the nut once you have done either of these things.

5. Repeat steps 2 through 4 to mount the three remaining eyebolts at the other marks you made.

6. Attach the chain to the eyebolts using the repair links. If necessary, push the bottoms of the A-frame together a bit to give yourself some slack. Leave three or four links hanging on one end.

Finishing the A-Frame

1. Cut the half sheet of plywood as shown in Figure 6. You will end up with nine squares, each 16" on a side.

2. Cut each square in half, diagonally, as also shown in Figure 6. The cuts don't have to be anywhere near perfect. These supports will be mounted on the underside of the A-frame, where almost no one will see them.

3. At each corner of the A-frame skeleton, where two 2x4s meet each other at right angles, mount a triangle with the right angle following the 2x4s and the hypotenuse hanging off into space. Clamp the triangle in place and drive in three screws, one in each corner of the triangle (see Figure 7). I put four or five #6 x 2" long dry wall screws on each of the two perpendicular sides for a total of seven to nine screws for each triangle.

NOTE: Make sure that the triangles don't interfere with the eyebolts on the frame.

4. If you are a Martha Stewart type, you will have painted a primer coat on the triangles before you started. I'm not that careful, so I painted them with a white exterior latex primer *after* mounting them.

5. The A-frame is now ready to stand on its own. Set it up and check the height at the apex. It should be 5'6" for AKC, NADAC, USDAA Performance, and USDAA 12" Championship division or 6'3" for all other USDAA Championship divisions. If it's not, either shorten the chain to raise it or lengthen the chain to lower it.

6. Cut the PVC to a length of 36" and place it in the groove made by the hinge in the A-frame. This will keep dogs from getting a paw caught in it.

7. The A-frame is now ready to paint. Disassemble it and lay the side walls flat with the plywood side up.

8. Paint the A-frame according to the instructions on page 98.

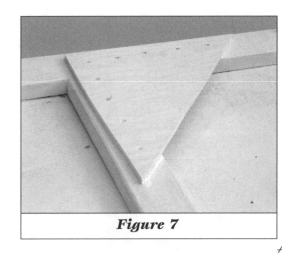

Figure 7

rejuvenating and refurbishing an a-frame

my obstacle plans have been around for about four years now. Each obstacle was built and tested before I wrote the plans. These proto-types range from total failures (like the A-frame skeleton made from PVC) to moderate successes. (The garbage collectors in my neigh-borhood think I'm insane.) One of my first prototypes was a wooden A-frame. But since I now have an aluminum A-frame, the wooden A-frame is folded up and propped against a tree in the backyard. However, with all of the questions I've gotten about renovating and refurbishing A-frames, this seemed like a good time to unearth the old prototype and give it a facelift. These plans describe that process.

Termites and Wood Damage

When I first moved the A-frame from where it had sat for two years, I noticed rotted wood along the bottom edges where they touched the ground. Rot is a way of life here in Mississippi, so I assumed it was wet rot, which is the decomposition of wood that's never allowed to dry out. But it was worse—termite damage. Termites are also all over this part of the country, so I shouldn't have been all that surprised.

I carefully removed the unsalvageable wood (just two 2x4s along the bottom edge) and sprayed the remaining wood (near the bottom part of the A-frame) with insecticide, according to the instructions on the bottle.

One of the new 2x4s became the base to hold the new retractable wheels (see next section). The wheels will allow me to move the A-frame around more frequently so that the termites don't have a chance to reestablish themselves.

Adding Wheels to the A-Frame

Do you know what is a lot easier than mounting wheels to your wooden A-frame? Buy a furniture dolly! Have someone help you lift one end of the A-frame onto the dolly, then you can lift the other side and move the A-frame around wheelbarrow-style. However, if you would rather mount permanent, retractable wheels onto your A-frame, then follow these steps.

Materials Needed

- 1 – 2" x 4" x 8' stud
- 2 – 4" utility hinges
  NOTE: Preferably, find some with removable pins.
- 4 – 3" swivel casters
  NOTE: I used 210 lb. test casters, but sturdier is better.
- 16 – $^1/_4$" x 1 $^1/_2$" lag screws
- 2 – #4 eye screws
- 1 – $^3/_8$" bolt snap hook
- 1 – $^1/_4$" x 4 $^1/_2$" carriage bolt
- 1 – $^1/_4$" fender washer
- 1 – $^1/_4$" wing nut

NOTE: You can substitute one or two C-clamps, pistol-grip adjustable clamps, or spring clamps for the last three items on the materials list—the carriage bolt, washer and wing nut. However, if you do, make sure the clamp is very strong and has a minimum span of 4 $^1/_2$" (see step 5 for more information).

Tools Needed

- Circular saw, PVC cutter, or hacksaw

- Drill with $^3/_{16}$" bit, $^5/_{16}$" bit that's 6" or longer, and screwdriver bit

- Ratcheting socket wrench with socket for lag screws. You can use an adjustable wrench or box wrench, but it will take much longer.

- Carpenter's ruler or tape measure

- Pencil or marker

Making the Wheels

1. Measure the inside width of your A-frame skeleton (that is, underneath the top surface of the obstacle between the pieces forming the sides of the frame/skeleton) and cut two pieces from the 2x4 to this length. My A-frame is made to AKC specifications and is 48" wide. It has 2x4s forming the sides of the frame with the *wide* side of each 2x4 against the plywood top. Since a 2x4 is actually 1 $^1/_2$" x 3 $^1/_2$", the inside width of my A-frame is 41".

2. Place one of the cut 2x4s on a workbench or sawhorses with the wider side of the board facing up. Position a caster at each end of the board. You can set the middle casters by eye or, if you're a per-

fectionist, you can measure. (Measure the distance between the two end casters and then measure the width of the mounting plates. Subtract the width of the two plates from the distance between the casters and divide this number by 3.) Once you have positioned four of the casters, use a pencil to mark the holes in the mounting plates. Drill a $^3/_{16}$" pilot hole at each mark and drive in lag screws to mount the plates. The finished unit should look like Figure 1.

3. The next step depends on how your A-frame is constructed.

   a. Since I was replacing the 2x4s on the bottom of my A-frame, I attached the 2x4 with the casters to one of these new 2x4s with the two utility hinges as shown in Figure 2. I mounted the caster assembly with two screws, then tested it to make sure the wheels would touch the ground when they were supposed to, but would be above the ground when retracted.

   b. If you can't attach the caster assembly directly to your A-frame in this way, take the other 2x4 piece you cut in step 1 and attach it to the 2x4 with the casters using the two utility hinges. You can use the screws that are provided with the hinges. Before attaching the hinges, be sure the assembly will not only lie flat on your workbench, but will also fold up so that the 2x4s

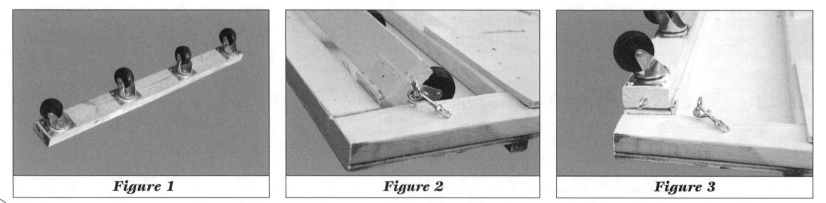

| *Figure 1* | *Figure 2* | *Figure 3* |

are parallel and lying one on top of the other with the wheels on top of the whole thing as shown in Figure 3. Mount this hinged assembly to one side of your A-frame, as close to the bottom edge of the frame as possible.

4. Drill a $^3/_{16}$" pilot hole and mount an eye screw in the cut end of the 2x4 with the casters. Then, retract the wheel assembly and make a mark where the eye screw ends up on the side of the A-frame. Drill a $^3/_{16}$" pilot hole here and mount a second eye screw. It's harder than you think, and you may need to move the second eye screw a bit. If you do, just fill the hole you left behind with wood putty; no one will notice your mistake after you paint over it. When you get it just right, the two eye screws will end up snug next to each other, and will not hit each other as the wheel assembly is moved into and out of position. Secure the wheel assembly in the retracted position with the snap hook. (See Figures 2 and 3 for guidance.)

5. Release the snap hook and set it aside. Now, you need some way to lock the wheels in the down position. Remember that the wheels will have to carry over 150 lbs., so safety is an issue here. I drilled a $^5/_{16}$" hole through both 2x4s and the plywood surface of the A-frame, then secured the wheels in the down position with a carriage bolt (with the head of the bolt underneath the A-frame), a fender washer (next to the plywood),

and a wing nut as shown in Figure 4. (A couple of sturdy C-clamps work just as well.) When the wheels are down, the weight of the A-frame is resting on the wheels and the two flat, parallel 2x4s.

Figure 4

Using the Wheels to Move the A-Frame

1. Before you move the A-frame, you need to set the wheels in the down position. To do this, you or an assistant can lift the A-frame several inches off the ground and "chock" the end so that it rests off the ground (two pieces of scrap 4x4 lumber or bricks are good for this purpose). Be very careful not to have the A-frame collapse onto your hands as you do this. Then, release the snap hook and let the wheels fall into the down position. Secure the wheels in this position with the carriage bolt (fed from underneath) or clamp the 2x4s together with a sturdy C-clamp.

2. Lift the A-frame slightly and remove the chocks, again being careful to protect your hands. Move around to the other side of the A-frame, lift it off the ground slightly, and wheel it to its new location as if it was a large, ungainly wheelbarrow.

   NOTE: You might find it easier to move the A-frame if you mount two eye screws on the underside of the non-wheeled end, then pass a circle of rope through these to provide you with a handle for moving the obstacle.

3. When the frame is in place, chock the side with the wheels, remove the bolt and wing nuts, and flip the wheels up into the retracted position. Secure them there with the snap hook. Remove the chocks and the A-frame is ready for action in its new location.

Updating Slats on an Old A-Frame

Before you go shopping for the materials listed below, please read "Making Climbing Slats" on page 97.

Once you've decided what type of new slats to use, you'll need to remove the old slats, prepare and mount the new ones, and then repaint and sand the obstacle.

Materials Needed

- 48 – linear feet of millwork

  NOTE: It's a good idea to buy some extra in case of accidents.

- 1 – box staples or brads that are about $^3/_8$" longer than the thickness of the slats

Tools Needed

- Versa-Bar
- Hammer
- Hacksaw or Dremel tool
- Circular saw
- Mitre saw or backsaw with the finest-toothed blade you can get

Figure 5

- C-clamps or pistol-grip adjustable clamps with at least a 3" span
- Staple gun or electric nail gun that takes selected staples or brads
- Carpenter's ruler or tape measure
- Pencil or marker
- Carpenter's glue (optional)

Removing the Old Slats

I use a Versa-Bar (see Figure 5) and a hammer to remove old slats. It helps to use a hacksaw or Dremel tool to cut part way through the slat so that it's easier to split where you want it to. Use the hammer to drive the Versa-Bar between the plywood and the slat. Then pry it up, breaking the slat (*not* the plywood) as you go. If necessary, you can patch small goofs with wood putty before attaching the new slats to your A-frame.

If nails or screws prove too difficult to remove, cut them off close to the plywood with a Dremel tool mounted with a cutoff wheel (be sure to wear eye protection for this task). The new slat will cover the rough edge that remains.

Mounting the New Slats

1. Cut the millwork for the climbing slats into strips using the mitre saw or backsaw. If you try to use an electric saw, the millwork will splinter and make a mess. It really needs to be cut by hand.

   NOTE: Rather than cutting the strips to the width of the A-frame, I cut them 1" longer than required (37" in this case). After mounting the strips, I use a circular saw to cut them flush to the A-frame edge.

2. Put one of the side walls on sawhorses or on a flat surface where you can work easily and have access to both sides at once. Position the slats on the top surface of the side wall so that the centers of the slats are spaced at 12" intervals with no slat falling within 4" of the top of the contact zone or the end of the frame. For each slat, be sure

to take a measurement on both edges of the A-frame wall so that you're sure the slats are straight. As you work, use a pencil to mark the position of each slat.

3. Either have an assistant hold a slat in place or clamp the slat to the plywood using C-clamps, spring clamps, or pistol-grip adjustable clamps. Mount the strips to the plywood wall of the A-frame using staples or brads (screws will split the delicate millwork), securing it every 3"-4". Repeat until you have mounted all of the slats on each side of the A-frame. If you don't have an assistant, you can just keep moving the clamps to the next slat.

    NOTE: If you cut the slats long as suggested, make the left edge flush with the left side of the A-frame and let the right edge hang over the other side of the A-frame. (Unless you are left-handed, in which case, reverse this.) If you want, you can place a thin layer of carpenter's glue on each slat before nailing or stapling it. However, if someone comes along and changes slat specifications next week, you'll be sorry you did this since the slats will be almost impossible to remove.

4. If you cut the slats long and let the ends of them hang over the edge of the A-frame, now is the time to trim them flush with the side of the A-frame using a circular saw or jigsaw. The slats will *not* split if you use an electric saw here because they are supported by the plywood and cannot flex.

5. Paint the A-frame according to the instructions on page 98.

Reinforcing the Frame/Skeleton

I found that my original design for the wooden A-frame produces a usable frame, but one that becomes weaker with time. To strengthen the frame without adding too much weight, I made corner supports like the one in Figure 6. The old frame flexed; the renovated frame is a lot stiffer and feels sturdier overall.

Materials Needed

- 1 – 4' x 4' half sheet $^1/_2$" plywood, CDX or marine grade
- 1 – box #6 x 2" galvanized exterior drywall screws
- Paint (flat white exterior latex)

Tools Needed

- Circular saw
- Drill with $^1/_8$" bit
- Power screwdriver or drill bit for Phillips-head screws
- C-clamps, spring clamps, or pistol-grip adjustable clamps
- Disposable mini-roller (4", 6", or 8") and 2" paintbrush
- Carpenter's ruler or tape measure
- Marker or pencil

Directions

1. Either have the home center where you buy the plywood cut it as shown in Figure 7, or take it home and cut it yourself. It doesn't have to be anywhere near perfect. You will end up with nine squares, each 16" on a side.

2. Cut each square in half, diagonally, as also shown in Figure 7. Again, the cuts don't have to be perfect. These supports will be mounted on the underside of the A-frame, where almost no one will see them.

3. At each corner of the A-frame skeleton, where two 2x4s meet each other at right angles, mount a triangle with the right angle following the 2x4s and the hypotenuse hanging off into space. Clamp the triangle in place and drive in three screws, one in each corner of the triangle. I put four or five screws on each of the two perpendicular sides for a total of seven to nine screws for each triangle.

NOTE: Make sure that the triangles don't interfere with something, like the wheels or the places where the chains bolt to the frame.

4. If you are a Martha Stewart type, you will have painted a primer coat on the triangles before you started. I'm not that careful, so I painted them with a white exterior latex primer *after* mounting them.

Replacing the Hinge

I didn't need to replace the hinge on my A-frame, but if I had, I would have switched to a continuous hinge as described in this section.

Materials Needed

- 1 – 36" continuous hinge, part #15665A429 from McMaster-Carr

  NOTE: This hinge is designed for welding, so you will need to drill screw holes for mounting it.

- 1 – box #6 x 1 $^1/_2$" wood screws, pan head or round head
- 1 – $^1/_4$" diameter *unthreaded* steel rod at least 3' long
- Drill with $^1/_8$", $^3/_{16}$", and $^1/_4$" bits
- Power screwdriver or drill bit for Phillips-head screws
- Dremel tool with cutoff wheel or hacksaw
- Bench vise
- Spring clamp to hold hinge and scrap wood (optional)
- Hammer and nail set
- Pliers
- Carpenter's ruler or tape measure
- Pencil or marker

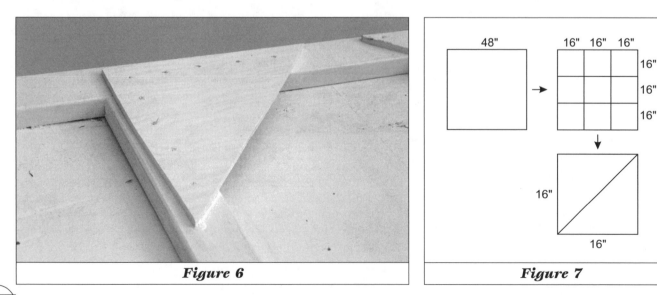

Figure 6

Figure 7

Directions

1. Place a scrap piece of wood on a sturdy, level surface. Clamp the hinge in place and drill holes at 4"-6" intervals in both sides of the hinge. You want the holes to be bigger than the shaft of the mounting screws, but not so big that the screw heads can slip through. Start with the smallest drill bits and work up to the larger ones—no one can drill a $1/4$" hole in thick steel without drilling a smaller hole first. The drill will just bind up.

   NOTE: After you drill several holes, you can use these to temporarily mount the hinge to your piece of scrap wood. This will make it easier to drill the remaining holes.

2. Cut the steel rod to 38". A Dremel tool is handy for this task (wear goggles), but a hacksaw will work as well.

3. Make a mark 2" from the end of the rod, then clamp the rod in a bench vise so that the mark is just visible at the edge of the jaws. Using your bare hands or a pair of pliers, bend the rod so that it makes an "L" shape with 2" of rod forming the short leg of the "L" and 36" forming the long leg.

4. Set the A-frame on a flat, level surface with the two sides forming an angle to each other—it should be in the same position as when it's used, but just on its side.

5. Have an assistant hold the frame in place while you remove the old hinge(s) holding it together. Then, take the new hinge, line it up so that it is correctly positioned, and drill $1/8$" pilot holes in four places. Drive four wood screws in place and then check to make sure everything is lined up right before continuing. If you made a mistake, you only have to remove four screws instead of a dozen or more. If everything seems right, then drill pilot holes for the remaining screws and drive the screws in place.

6. Rest the A-frame flat on the ground so that you could walk on it if you wanted to. Using a hammer and a nail, drive the hinge pin out of the hinge. Replace the hinge pin with the bent $1/4$" steel rod. In use, you should point the "handle" part of the rod toward the ground so that it does not present a potential hazard.

Now you're ready to train on your almost new A-frame!

W̶elded aluminum or steel dogwalk

these plans are for having dogwalk bases welded from tubular aluminum or steel. The dogwalk needs a little more woodworking than the welded A-frame to finish it off.

Simplifying Your Life

One easy way around the issue of welding dogwalk bases is to buy bases from MAX 200/Pipe Dreams or one of the other companies listed in the "Resource Guide." If you are teaching classes, the MAX 200 bases are nice since they collapse down to ground level for teaching rookies and rise up to regulation height. That's what I use, both in my backyard and at the training school. The drawback of purchasing bases is the cost of shipping. The bases are too large to go by UPS, so they must be delivered by motor freight, which is neither convenient nor cheap.

These plans include professionally-drawn blueprints for getting bases welded. Just choose the material you want to use—aluminum or steel—and then take the appropriate plans to a welder. Each base weighs only 15 lbs. when made from aluminum.

Choosing the Materials

You have two choices of materials for dogwalk bases: steel or aluminum. Following is a summary of their advantages and disadvantages.

	Aluminum	Steel
Weight	Light	Heavy
Cost	Expensive	Cheap
Finding a welder	Difficult	Easy
Weather-resistance	Excellent	Very poor

Finding a Welding Shop

For tips on finding a local welder, see page 99 earlier in this chapter. The cost for having these dogwalk bases welded locally was $265 each ($530 for the pair). Expect to pay another $100 for lumber and materials.

Preparing the Middle Plank

I recommend pressure-treated 2x12 lumber for the dogwalk planks. You can scrimp and use 1x12s, but the dogwalk will not last long outdoors and will bounce noticeably.

Materials Needed

- 3 – 2" x 12" x 12' pressure-treated planks
- 4 – 4" door hinges or utility hinges with *removable* pins

  NOTE: Alternatively, buy a 36" continuous hinge from McMaster-Carr (#15665A429). Ask your welder to cut it into 11" pieces and drill $1/4$" holes at 2" intervals. This type of hinge doesn't need to be lined up as described in steps 5 and 6. However, you still need to make an L-shaped pin from the steel rod as described in "Adding the Up and Down Ramps." This rod will replace the hinge pin that come with the continuous hinge, but can be removed easily when you are breaking down the dogwalk to move it.

- 1 – $3/16$" diameter *unthreaded* steel rod at least 3' long

contact obstacles

- 8 – $^1/_4$" x 3" carriage bolts
- 8 – $^1/_4$" hex nuts with lock washers to fit

  OR

- 8 – $^1/_4$" wing nuts

  NOTE: Hex nuts are better for a permanent construction, while wing nuts allow you to remove the plank, if necessary.

Tools Needed

- Drill with $^1/_4$" and $^3/_{32}$" bits
- Power screwdriver or drill bit for Phillips-head screws
- C-clamps, spring clamps, or pistol-grip adjustable clamps
- Socket wrench or nut driver to fit $^1/_4$" nuts purchased above or pliers if wing nuts used
- Carpenter's ruler or tape measure
- Pencil or marker

Directions

You will only use one of the 12' long planks to complete the steps in this section; the other two will form the up and down ramps of your dog-walk (see next section). Set them aside for now.

1. Measure 3' from the end of the plank and make a mark across the width of the plank. Repeat for the other side of the plank. These marks should be about 6' apart.

2. Set up the welded bases about 6' apart. With the help of an assistant, lift the plank so that it rests on the top plates of the bases. Shift the plank or the bases so that each mark lines up with the center of a base. Measure from underneath to make sure the plates are centered on the width of the plank. Write "bottom" on the underside of the plank, and "top" on the top side (that is, the surface the dogs will walk on when you are done). When you are confident everything is where you want it, clamp the plank to the top plates using the C-clamps or spring clamps.

3. The plate attached to each base has four holes drilled in it by the machine shop. Working from underneath, and using the $^1/_4$" bit, drill up through the plank using each hole as a guide. You'll drill a total of eight holes.

4. Flip over the plank so that the side marked "bottom" is now facing up and clamp it in place on the bases as before.

5. Clamp two of the door hinges to one end of the plank. Space them evenly along the width of the plank. Make sure the rounded "knuckle" of the hinge (the part that holds the pin in place) is flush with the edge of the plank as shown in the photo below. Also make sure the hinge pin "heads" are on the outside edges of the plank so that you will have access to them when needed. Clamp the hinges in place.

6. Drill pilot holes with the $^3/_{32}$" bit. Using the screws provided, mount one side of the hinges to the plank. If the clamps are in your way, drive in one or two screws to hold the hinge in place, then remove the clamps and drive in the remaining screws.

7. Repeat steps 5 and 6 at the other end of the plank with the remaining two door hinges.

8. Now, flip over the plank on the bases so that the side marked "top" is facing up. Line up the holes you drilled in step 3 with the holes in the plates on the bases. For each hole, feed a carriage bolt down through the wood and then the metal plate.

9. If you purchased hex nuts, thread a lock washer on the end of each bolt and then a hex nut. Tighten with a socket wrench or nut driver. If you are using wing nuts, omit the lock washers and tighten the wing nuts with pliers. When the bolts are tightened, you want the bolt heads to barely protrude above the surface of the wood. Use a hammer to drive the bolts into the surface of the wood if necessary.

contact obstacles

Adding the Up and Down Ramps

You will use the two 12' long planks you set aside to complete the steps in this section.

Tools Needed

- Drill with $3/32$" bit
- Pliers
- Sawhorse
- Goggles
- Dremel tool with cutoff wheel or hacksaw
- Bench vise
- Carpenter's ruler or tape measure
- Pencil or marker

Directions

1. Now you need to attach ramps to your middle plank. Take one of the remaining planks and place it so that it's end to end with the plank on the dogwalk bases. Either have an assistant hold the plank in place or prop it on a sawhorse so that it stays in place—the plank is heavy and you want to make sure that it will not fall on you.

2. Line up the opposite sides of the hinges already mounted to the middle plank on the new ramp plank. When the hinges are positioned as desired, clamp them to the ramp plank. Drill pilot holes with the $3/32$" bit and mount the other side of the hinges using the screws provided with the hinges.

   NOTE: A slight gap between the ramp plank and the middle plank is normal and needed to accommodate the knuckle of the hinge.

3. Repeat steps 1 and 2 to attach the remaining ramp plank to the other side of the middle plank.

4. Measure 14" from each end of the 36" unthreaded steel rod and make a mark. Wearing goggles, use these marks as a guide to cut through the rod with a Dremel tool or hacksaw. File the cut edges so they're smooth.

5. Measure 10 $3/4$" from the end of one of the cut pieces of rod and make a mark. Clamp the rod in the bench vise with the jaw of the vise where you made the mark. Bend the rod at a right angle. Repeat for the other piece of rod. You now have two L-shaped pieces, with the short arm of the L about 3" and the long arm about 10 $3/4$".

6. Starting with either ramp, make sure it is well supported—either by a sawhorse or by an assistant—and remove the hinge pins on that side with pliers. (Penetrating oil sprayed into the hinge will help.) Replace the hinge pins with one of the L-shaped pieces of rod you made. The long side goes where the hinge pins once lived and the short side should point downward so it doesn't snag on anything. Repeat to replace the hinge pins on the other side of the dogwalk.

You can now remove the ramps to store or move the dogwalk. Just support each ramp, one at a time, and pull the pin.

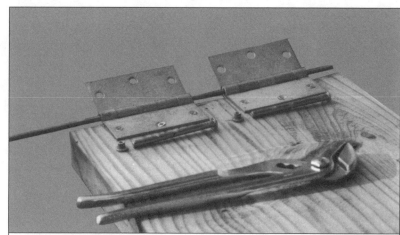

Hinges Attached to Middle Plank of Dogwalk

Attaching Slats and Painting

Before you go shopping for the materials listed below, please read "Making Climbing Slats" on page 97.

Materials Needed

- 24 – linear feet of millwork

  NOTE: It's a good idea to buy some extra in case of accidents.

- 1 – box staples or brads that are about $^3/_8$" longer than the thickness of the slats

Tools Needed

- Circular saw
- Mitre saw or backsaw with the finest-toothed blade you can get
- C-clamps, spring clamps, or pistol-grip adjustable clamps
- Staple gun or electric nail gun that takes selected staples or brads
- Carpenter's ruler or tape measure
- Pencil or marker
- Carpenter's glue (optional)

Directions

1. Cut the millwork into 12" long strips using the mitre saw or backsaw. If you try to use an electric saw, the millwork will splinter and make a mess. It needs to be cut by hand.

   NOTE: Rather than cutting the strips to the exact width of the planks, I cut 1" longer than needed (13" in this case), mount the strips as described in the steps below, and then use a circular saw or jigsaw to cut the strips flush with the edge of the planks.

2. You will mount slats to the up and down ramps (the middle plank does not have slats). Starting 12" from the bottom of the ramp, position the slats on the ramp so that the centers of the slats are spaced at 12" intervals with no slat falling within 4" of the top of the contact zone (42" from the end of the plank for an AKC dogwalk or 36" from the end of the plank for a USDAA/NADAC dogwalk) or the end of the ramp. For each slat, take a measurement on both edges of the ramp so that you're sure the slats are straight. As you work, use a pencil to mark the position of each slat.

3. Have an assistant hold a slat in place or clamp the slat to the plywood using C-clamps, spring clamps, or pistol-grip adjustable clamps. Mount each slat using staples or brads (screws will split the delicate millwork). Secure each slat every 3"-4". Repeat until you have mounted all of the slats on each ramp. If you don't have an assistant, you can just keep moving the clamps to the next slat.

   NOTE: If you cut the slats long, as suggested in step 1, make the left edge flush with the left side of the ramp and let the right edge hang over the other side of the ramp. (Unless you are left-handed, in which case, reverse this.) If you want, you can place a thin layer of carpenter's glue on each slat before nailing or stapling it. However, if someone comes along and changes slat specifications next week, you'll be sorry you did this since the slats will be almost impossible to remove.

4. If you cut the slats long and let the ends of them hang over the edge of the planks, now is the time to trim them flush with the side of the planks using a circular saw or jigsaw. The slats will *not* split if you use an electric saw here because they are supported by the wood and cannot flex.

5. Paint the finished dogwalk planks according to the instructions on page 98.

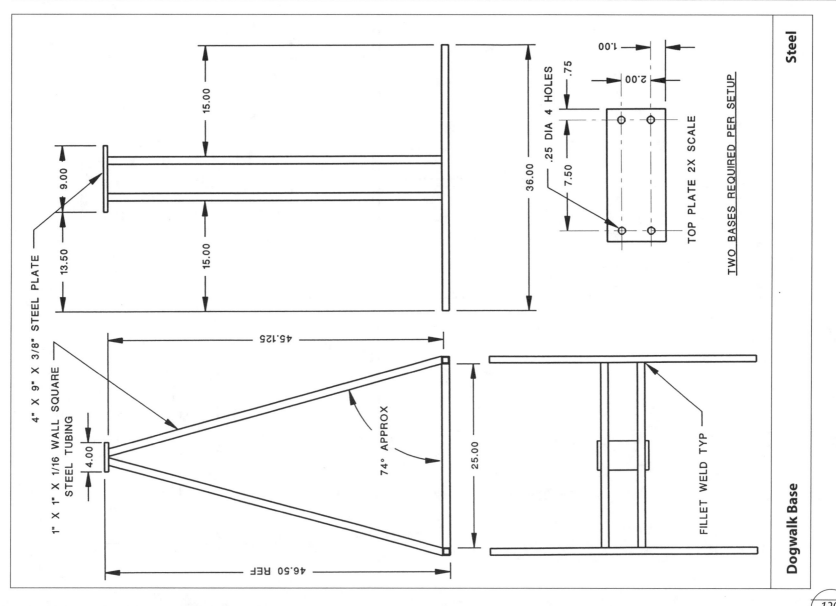

9.00

15.00

15.00

36.00

13.50

4" X 9" X 3/8" STEEL PLATE

.25 DIA 4 HOLES

7.50

1.00

2.00

.75

TOP PLATE 2X SCALE

TWO BASES REQUIRED PER SETUP

45.125

4.00

74° APPROX

25.00

46.50 REF

1" X 1" X 1/16 WALL SQUARE
STEEL TUBING

FILLET WELD TYP

Dogwalk Base

contact obstacles

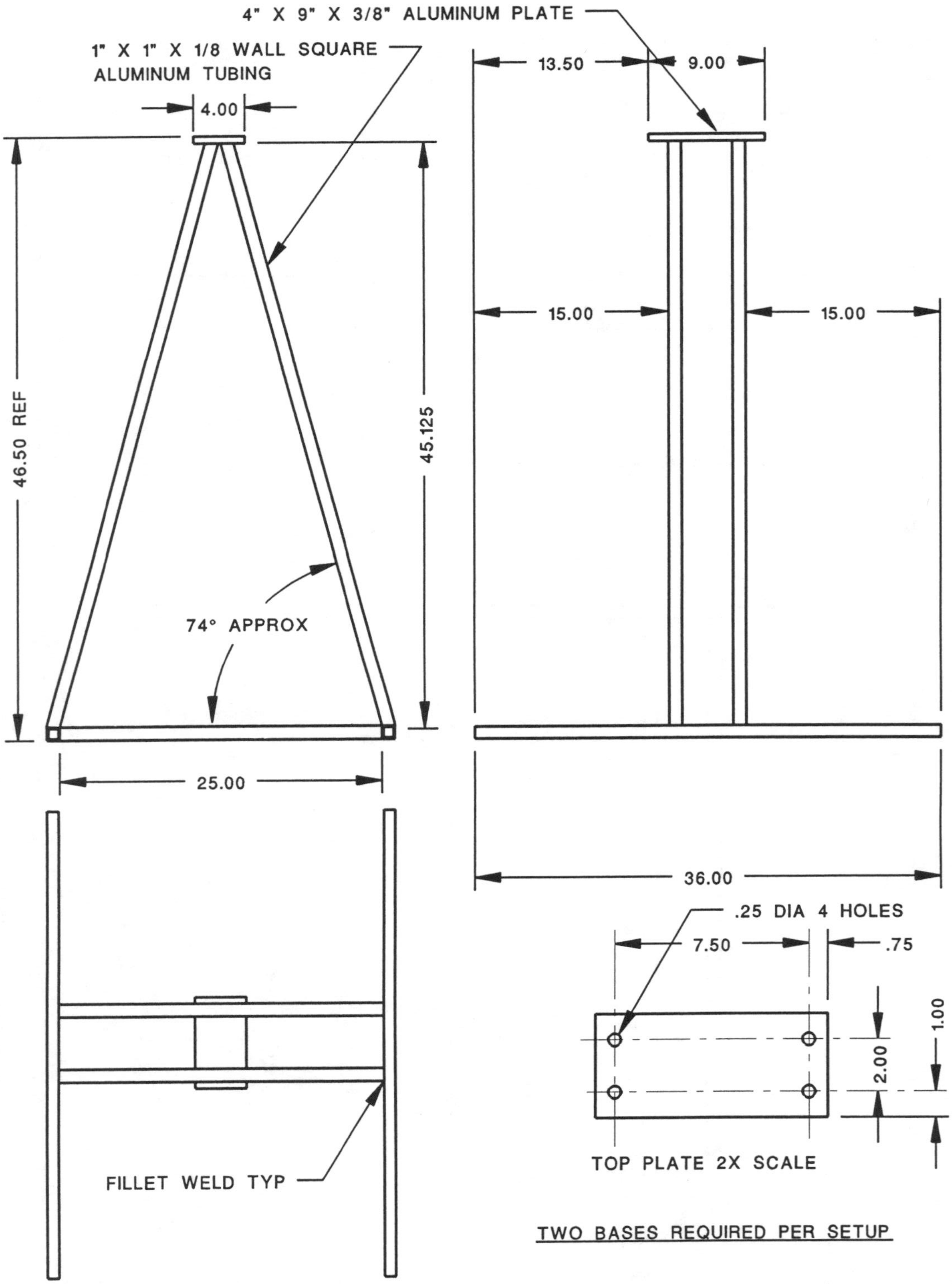

4" X 9" X 3/8" ALUMINUM PLATE

15.00

9.00

13.50

15.00

36.00

.25 DIA 4 HOLES

.75

1.00

2.00

7.50

TOP PLATE 2X SCALE

TWO BASES REQUIRED PER SETUP

Aluminum

1" X 1" X 1/8 WALL SQUARE
ALUMINUM TUBING

4.00

45.125

74° APPROX

25.00

46.50 REF

FILLET WELD TYP

Dogwalk Base

# *a*djustable seesaw

t hese plans are for an adjustable seesaw which is legal for competition, but can also be used at lower heights for training. The seesaw weighs about 75 lbs.—I prefer a rock-solid seesaw base that does not move around when a Mastiff goes over it. The cost for constructing this seesaw ranges from $50-$100, depending on whether you have paint and similar supplies on hand or have to buy them.

NOTE: If you would prefer to make a seesaw that is not adjustable, modify the materials list so that you only purchase two of the flush bushings and two rubber stoppers. Only drill the top hole shown in Figures 4, 5, and 6. Everything else is the same.

Materials Needed

- 1 – 4' x 4' half sheet ¹⁵/₈" or ³/₄" plywood, CDX or marine grade

- 1 – 2" x 12" x 12' pressure-treated board

- 1 – 2" x 12" x 8' pressure-treated board

  NOTE: Less than a 2' length is needed, so if you can find a scrap piece, use it. Or, if you don't mind dealing with a very long, heavy board, you can buy a 2" x 12" x 14' board instead of the 2" x 12" x 12' and cut it down. This will give you the extra 2' piece you need.

- 2 – 2" x 4" x 8' pressure-treated board

- 1 – ³/₄" diameter aluminum rod, 24" long

  NOTE: Available from Small Parts Inc., part #E-ZRA-12-24.

- 4 – ¹/₄" x 6" carriage bolts

- 4 – ¹/₄" wing nuts

- 1 – ³/₄" SDR 21 PVC pipe, scrap or new, 24" long

  NOTE: This pipe has thinner walls than Schedule 40 pipe. But, if you can't find it, use 1" schedule 40 PVC pipe.

- 8 – ³/₄" x 1" schedule 40 PVC flush bushings

  NOTE: These should have threads to hold ³/₄" galvanized pipe on one end and a 1" PVC slip fitting on the other end as shown in Figure 1. Outer diameter "A" depends on manufacturer.

- 8 – threaded PVC plugs to fit the PVC flush bushings

- 1 – box #6 x 2" galvanized exterior drywall screws

- 1 – box #6 x 3" galvanized exterior drywall screws

- 2 – tubes exterior caulk

  NOTE: I prefer the brand called "Alex." It's durable and can be painted.

- Wood putty

- Carpenter's glue

- 8 – #5 rubber stoppers

  NOTE: These are optional; see "Painting and Finishing the Seesaw" for more information.

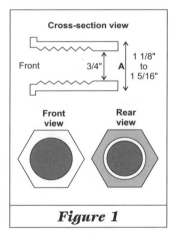

Figure 1

Cross-section view

Front   3/4"   A   1 1/8" to 1 5/16"

Front view   Rear view

contact obstacles

Tools Needed

- Circular saw
- Drill with the following bits: $1/4$" drill bit, extra-long (more than 6"); a Forstner-type drill bit or hole saw to match the diameter of flush bushings (dimension "A" in Figure 1); and a Phillips-head screwdriver bit to fit the drywall screws.
- Router with $3/4$" dado bit
- Power screwdriver
- Caulk gun
- Dremel tool with cutting wheel (or hacksaw)
- Safety goggles
- Clamps with at least 5" grip or pipe clamps
- Carpenter's ruler or tape measure
- Pencil or marker

Making the Two Sides of the Base

1. Cut the plywood sheet into a square that is 35 $1/2$" on each side.

2. Draw two diagonal lines to the opposite corners of the square as shown in Figure 2. These lines will be about 50" long. Then cut along one of the lines to divide the square into two identical triangles. Each one of these will be a side of the seesaw base. (You will use the second line you marked later on.)

3. Cut the 90° corner off each triangle. To determine where to cut, draw a line 5 $1/2$" long that is parallel to the long side of the triangle as shown in Figure 3.

4. Measure down 1 $3/4$" from the last cut, following the second line you made in step 2. This is the center line of the side of the base. Make a mark as shown in Figure 4. Keep making tick marks at 4" intervals (5 $3/4$", 9 $3/4$", and 13 $3/4$") along the same center line. Repeat for the other side of the base. These marks will allow the seesaw to be adjusted to an apex of 24", 20", 16", and 12".

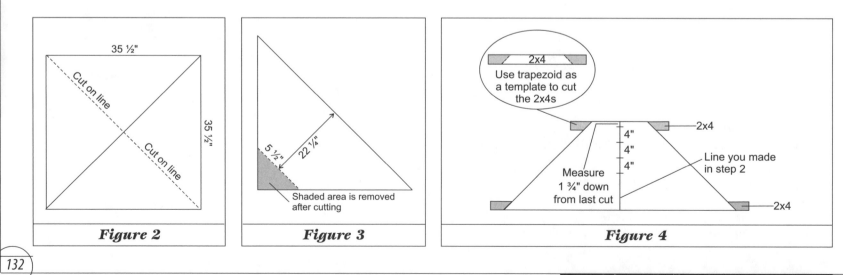

Figure 2 — 35 ½", 35 ½", Cut on line, Cut on line

Figure 3 — 5 ½", 22 ¼", Shaded area is removed after cutting

Figure 4 — Use trapezoid as a template to cut the 2x4s, 2x4, 2x4, 4", 4", 4", Line you made in step 2, Measure 1 ¾" down from last cut, 2x4, 2x4

contact obstacles

5. Cut a 2x4 piece that is 6" longer than the bottom edge of the plywood trapezoid and another piece that is 6" longer than the top edge. Place these pieces behind the plywood as shown in Figure 4 and draw lines on them using the angled sides of the plywood as a template. Cut the 2x4s along these lines and mount them to the plywood with 2" drywall screws so that all edges are flush. Do not put any screws within 1" of the tick marks you made. Repeat for the other side of the base.

6. Cut two 13" long pieces from the 2x4 lumber. Place one of the pieces at a right angle to the top 2x4 on each base, forming a "T," as shown in Figure 5. Drive 2" drywall screws into each 2x4 piece, being careful not to drive screws within 1" of the tick marks you made.

7. Using the Forstner-type drill bit or hole saw, drill holes that match the diameter of the flush bushings (diameter "A" in Figure 1). The tick marks you made along the center guide line are the center marks for the drill bit. Drill the holes as straight as possible (use a drill press if one is available), going through the plywood and the T-shaped 2x4 assembly as shown in Figure 5. Repeat for the other side of the base.

8. Screw a plug into each bushing. Then, using a C-clamp or pipe clamp, drive a PVC bushing into each hole you have made, working from the front side of the assembly (the one *without* the 2x4s) as shown in Figure 6. The threaded part of the fitting goes to the front (outside), while the smooth part which will carry the aluminum rod goes toward the back (inside). If necessary, ream out the hole a bit with the Dremel tool and a sander disk to make the bushing fit, but be sure it is tight. Repeat for the other side of the base.

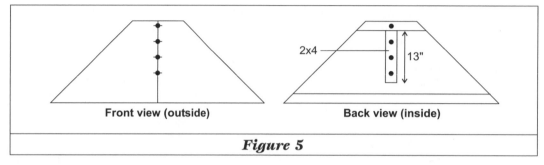

Figure 5

Making the Axle and Axle Housing

1. Cut the aluminum rod to a length of 15 $\frac{1}{2}$" with a hacksaw or Dremel tool. A hacksaw will take forever, but you can use the time to dream about how much easier life would be if you had a Dremel tool! Be sure to wear goggles. Aluminum shards in your eye are no fun at all.

2. Cut an 11 $\frac{1}{2}$" piece of PVC pipe. The PVC pipe should fit loosely over the aluminum rod you just cut so that the rod has room to move but doesn't rattle around. If it does not fit correctly, try using a different diameter PVC. Pipe from different manufacturers does vary in interior size so you may need to experiment.

3. Cut two $\frac{1}{2}$" pieces from the PVC pipe and set them aside. You won't need them until the final steps of completing the seesaw.

4. Cut two 11 $\frac{1}{2}$" pieces from the 2x4s.

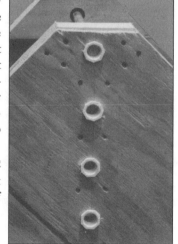

Figure 6

5. Measure the outside diameter of the PVC you cut in steps 2 and 3. You need to mark two parallel lines this distance apart on each of the 2x4 pieces you cut. For example, if you used ³/₄" SDR 21 PVC, the outside diameter is 1". Therefore, you would mark two parallel lines, 1" apart, centered along the length of the 2x4 as in Figure 7. If you measure 1 ¹/₄" from each edge of the board, the lines should be 1" apart.

6. Using a router and ³/₄" dado bit, rout out the center of each of the 11 ¹/₂" long 2x4 pieces to a depth of ¹/₂". This will take at least two passes in each direction (width and depth). It will be much easier if you can clamp the 2x4 to a work surface and clamp a parallel board onto a 2x4 scrap to guide your cuts.

7. Clamp the routed out 2x4s together with the 11 ¹/₂" PVC pipe sandwiched in between as shown in Figure 8. The PVC should fit very tightly and there shouldn't be any space between the boards when you are through. Re-rout or adjust as necessary to get the correct fit.

8. Unclamp the PVC pipe and 2x4s. Starting with either of the 2x4s, lay an ample amount of caulk in the routed groove. Place the PVC pipe inside, making sure that most of the space between the square groove and the circular pipe is filled with caulk. Don't worry about caulk oozing out. Lay an equal amount of caulk inside the other 2x4. Put wood glue on the surfaces of the 2x4s that will be touching and clamp the whole thing together again. Clean any excess caulk from the inside of the pipe. Any caulk left on the wood will not affect functionality, and you can always cut it off with a utility knife after it sets.

9. Secure the assembly with drywall screws if you want, and leave it clamped overnight to allow the glue and caulk to set properly.

This is the axle and axle housing.

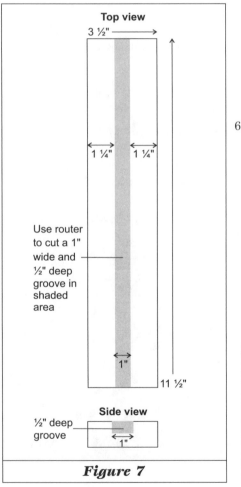

Top view

3 ½"

1 ¼"   1 ¼"

Use router to cut a 1" wide and ½" deep groove in shaded area

1"

11 ½"

Side view

½" deep groove

1"

Figure 7

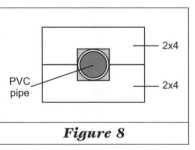

PVC pipe

2x4

2x4

Figure 8

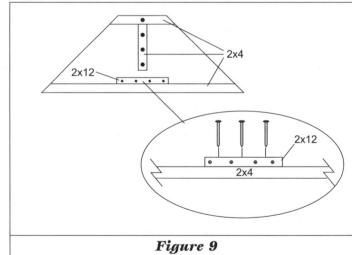

2x4

2x12

2x12

2x4

Figure 9

contact obstacles

Assembling the Base

While the caulk and glue are setting, complete the seesaw base.

1. Cut a 15" long piece from the 2x12 board. Place this piece so that it rests on the bottom 2x4 inside both sides of the seesaw base. Position it so that it's centered underneath the top 2x4 "T" as shown in Figure 9. (Note that the 12" wide ends of the 2x12 piece should be against the plywood sides of the base.)

2. Thread the aluminum rod through each set of holes in the two sides of the base to make sure they're properly aligned. Check and double-check this, then either clamp this assembly together with pipe clamps or have an assistant hold it for you.

3. On each side of the base, drill four pilot holes through the plywood and into the cut end of the 2x12. Drive a 3" drywall screw into each hole.

4. On each side of the 2x12, drive in three 3" drywall screws from above (angling them if you need to) through the top of the 2x12 and into the side of the 2x4 it's resting on.

Making the Plank

When the caulk and glue have set, prepare the 2" x 12" x 12' which will be the seesaw plank. You need to measure the board for mounting the axle housing. The housing is placed off-center so that the board tips.

1. Double-check the length of the board; it should be 144" long. Cut it down if required. If it's a little shorter, you'll need to adjust the measurements in the next step.

2. Divide the length of the board in half and then subtract 1". For a 144" long board this will be 71". Measure this distance from one end of the board and draw a line perpendicular to the length of the board at this point. The line will be 71" from one end of the board and 73" from the other end of the board as shown in Figure 10. The 73" side is the longer, heavier end and will be the "down" side of the seesaw plank (that is, the side that rests on the ground).

3. Measure 1 ³/₄" from each side of this line and draw another line perpendicular to the length of the board.

4. Using these lines as guides, clamp the 2x4 and PVC pipe assembly onto the 12' long board. Attach it to the board using 3" drywall screws as shown in Figure 11. Drive in the screws as deep as possible since you are working from what will be the top surface of the board.

5. Fill the tops of the screw holes with wood putty and smooth off with a putty knife or your finger.

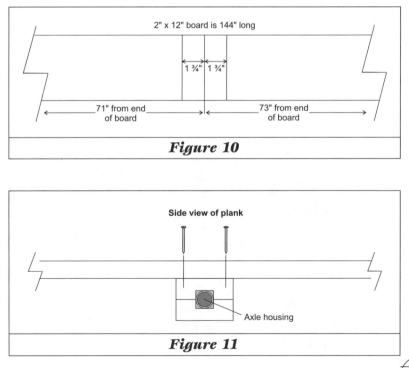

2" x 12" board is 144" long

1 ¾" 1 ¾"

71" from end of board   73" from end of board

Figure 10

Side view of plank

Axle housing

Figure 11

Final Assembly and Testing

- Assemble the seesaw: Have a helper rest one end of the plank on the ground and hold the other end in the air so that the hole in the axle assembly lines up with the holes in the base. Then insert the aluminum rod through the base and the axle assembly. Make sure the plank tips correctly and smoothly returns to resting position.

- If you are building an AKC seesaw, be aware of the *3-lb./3-second rule:* a 3 lb. weight placed 12" from the end of the plank must drop the board in 3 seconds. If this doesn't happen, you may have made the PVC pipe "collar" too tight on the aluminum rod. If this is the case, buy a $^5/_8$" diameter rod and cut it to fit rather than rebuilding the axle assembly. Greasing the rod and collar might help, too.

- Should you mount climbing slats on the plank? I prefer *not* to have slats on the seesaw, and most seesaws you see in competition are slatless.

- Mark two contact zones on the plank. Measure 36" from each end for a NADAC or USDAA seesaw or 42" for an AKC seesaw.

- If you're going to leave the seesaw outside, you may want to run a bead of caulk on the seams between the wood (for example, between the 2x4s and the plywood) before painting.

Painting and Finishing the Seesaw

1. Paint the seesaw according to the instructions on page 98.

2. After painting, make four "feet" for the base out of 4" to 6" long scrap pieces of pressure-treated 2x4. Mount them on the bottom of the base with the 6" carriage bolts and wing nuts. The head of the bolt should be near the ground, with the wing nut inside the seesaw base. The feet raise the base out of the dirt to protect the wood. They are easily replaced or removed, if necessary. After attaching the feet, make sure the apex of the seesaw is at the correct height (22-26" AKC, 24" NADAC, 24"-27" USDAA). If not, you can modify the feet to bring the base to specs.

3. The $^1/_2$" pieces of PVC pipe you cut in "Making the Axle and Axle Housing" are used to keep the plank from touching the inside surface of the base. You need at least $^1/_4$" clearance between the edge of the plank and the base: too small a space and you get friction; too large and a dog's paw might get caught. Thread the aluminum rod through the base and axle assembly, placing one of the $^1/_2$" long pieces of PVC pipe over the rod on each side of the axle assembly.

4. (Optional) Put a #5 rubber stopper in each of the PVC flush bushings to keep out dirt and moisture. Alternatively, threaded $^3/_4$" PVC plugs can be screwed into the bushings (if you didn't damage the bushings too much putting them into the base). Anything soft and about the right size will work. Just be sure whatever you use doesn't protrude so much that it's a hazard.

The number one question I'm asked about these plans is regarding the fit between the flush bushings and the aluminum axle. No, it's *not* supposed to be very tight. You want to be able to remove the axle and reset it at different heights.

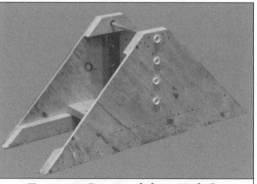

Base at Competition Height

Base at a Training Height

136

Contact training hoops

you can make hoops for training contact zones quickly and easily.

Materials Needed

- 2 – hula hoops
- 1 – 10' length $1/2$" schedule 40 PVC pipe
- 4 – $1/2$" PVC 4-way crosses
- 4 – $1/2$" PVC 45° elbows
- PVC cement

Tools Needed

- Hacksaw or Dremel tool
- PVC cutters (optional)

Directions

1. Cut the following pieces from the $1/2$" PVC:

   2 – 13 $1/2$" long
   4 – 2 $1/2$" long
   8 – 6" long

2. Cut the hula hoop in one place. Be careful not to drop the little ball bearings which make the neat-o "shick, shick" sound—they are a hazard if you lose them. Just collect and discard these.

3. Assemble the PVC pipe and parts for the base as shown in Figure 1.

   Do *not* glue anything yet!

4. Place the ends of the cut hula hoop in the open ends of the 45° elbows. Make sure the elbows are aligned so that they are perfectly straight.

5. When everything is aligned correctly, glue the parts of the base together. You can glue the hula hoop to the base, but it's not necessary.

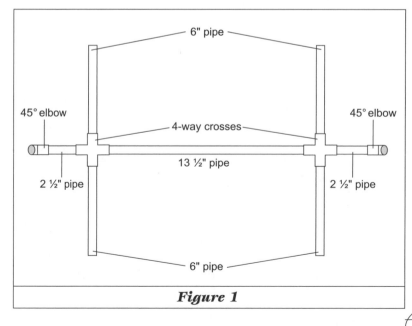

Figure 1

hapter four

Table and Weave Poles

Some notes on the pause table and weave poles:

- The pause table is an AKC and USDAA obstacle. It is not used in NADAC.
- Like constructing contact obstacles with slats that meet the requirements of all three organizations, building one set of weave poles that can be used in AKC, NADAC, and USDAA trials is a challenge and requires compromise.

Table Heights

The following chart shows the table height used for each jump height in AKC and USDAA at the time of this printing. This information is provided only as a reference for your convenience. Most of the organizations have up-to-date copies of their rulebooks or equipment specifications on their websites.

AKC Regular Classes

Jump Height	Table Height
8"	8"
12"	8"
16"	16"
20"	16"
24"	24"

USDAA Championship Classes

Jump Height	Table Height
12"	12"
16"	12" or 16"
22"	24"
26"	24"

AKC Preferred Classes

Jump Height	Table Height
4"	8"
8"	8"
12"	8"
16"	16"
20"	16"

USDAA Performance Classes

Jump Height	Table Height
8"	12"
12"	12"
16"	16"
22"	16"

Weave Pole Specifications

Changes in the AKC regulations for weave pole construction (effective as of September 2002) mean that many individuals and clubs will have to switch from spring-based weave poles to rigid weave poles. Rigid poles mounted on a base will now be the only kind allowed. (The regulations stipulate that stick in the ground poles may be used in an "emergency," but it's hard for me to envision an agility emergency.)

Another change is a recommended spacing between poles of 22". For years, I've been using 20" spacing. I prefer this for a lot of reasons, especially because you can buy 10' boards that don't need cutting for your bases. For the 22" spacing, you need 11' long bases, which means cutting down a 12' board. I also prefer to train on the narrower spacing (20") and trial at whatever gets thrown at me.

The new regulations also allow the use of 9-12 weave poles in the AKC Excellent classes. So you might consider making a set of two, three, or four weave poles in addition to the two sets of six specified in the plans included in this chapter. That way, you can make any number of weave poles from 8 to 16 for practice or trials.

A summary of each organization's requirements for the individual poles, as well as the base of the obstacle, is included here. If you need to build a set of weave poles that can be used in AKC, NADAC, and USDAA trials, you will have to compromise on the spacing between poles and build your weave poles with 21" between poles. ³/₄" schedule 40 PVC will be your best choice for making the poles.

Organization	Diameter of Poles	Length of Poles	Spacing Between Poles on Center
AKC	1"-1 ¹/₄"	36" min.	20"-24" (22" preferred)
NADAC/ASCA	³/₄"-1"	36"-48"	20"-21"
USDAA	1"	36"-48"	18"-21"

Organization	Height of Base	Width of Base
AKC	³/₄"	4"
NADAC/ASCA	³/₄"	4"
USDAA	1"	3 ¹/₂"

AKC rules also specify that the weave poles must have a fixed base with a rigid upright to support the pole. This upright must be no more than 4" high when measured from the ground to the top of the rigid support.

Plans Included

In this section, you will find the following plans:

- Pause Table
- Simple Indoor/Outdoor Weave Poles
- Indoor/Outdoor Weave Poles for Competition
- Training Weave Poles

ause table

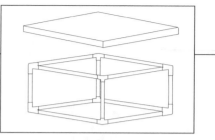

i t doesn't take very much time, or many materials, to make a table that is sturdy, versatile, and useful for practice or competition. These plans produce an extremely sturdy table that can be used for dogs of all heights, weights, and energy levels. Don't skimp on the size of the PVC though. If you use smaller diameter PVC than what's called for in the materials list (1 ½" PVC), the table will be rickety.

NOTE: If you are going to use the table for trials, it's a good idea to build two sets of bases. Then, the ring crew can be changing the height on one base outside the ring while the other base is in use in the ring. When there's a jump height change, the new base can be swapped for the old one in seconds.

Materials Needed

- 1 – half-sheet (48" x 48") ½" CDX plywood
- 2 – 2" x 4" x 8' framing lumber (studs)
- 2 to 4 – 10' lengths 1 ½" Schedule 40 PVC

  NOTE: If the table is to be used only at 8", you need two 10' lengths. If the table is to be used at any other single height, you need three 10' lengths. If you want to be able to adjust the table to the complete range of table heights for AKC or USDAA, you need four 10' lengths.

- 8 – 1 ½" PVC 3-way ells

  NOTE: The 3-way ells are a special part not found in home centers or plumbing supply stores. They must be ordered from one of the vendors listed in the "Resource Guide" at the beginning of this book under "Furniture-Grade PVC Pipe and Parts."

- 1 – box #8 x 2" exterior drywall screws, fine thread
- 1 – box #8 x 3" exterior drywall screws, fine thread
- 1 – bag play sand

  OR

- 1 – container of Skid-Tex

  NOTE: Some other additives for creating a good, nonslip surface on the contacts are Skid-Free, No-Skid, and Deck-Tec.

- PVC cement
- White primer paint
- Whatever color paint you want for the final coat on the table top
- (Optional) Tube exterior caulk, any color

Tools Needed

- Circular saw or table saw
- Drill with ¹/₁₆" bit
- Power screwdriver or drill with driver bits
- Hacksaw, Dremel tool with heavy-duty cutting wheel, or pipe cutter that can handle 1 ½" pipe
- 2" paintbrush
- Disposable 4" or 6" mini-rollers with two or three extra rollers
- Disposable paint trays
- Kitchen strainer with a window screen-like basket
- Caulk gun (if caulk is used)
- Carpenter's ruler or tape measure
- Pencil or marker

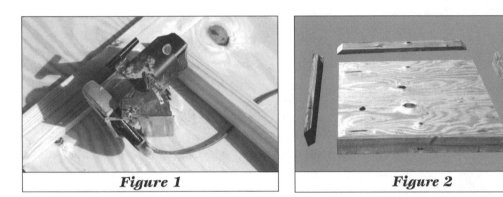

Figure 1

Figure 2

Making the Table Top

1. Carefully measure and mark a 36" square from the CDX plywood for the table top. If you select the two best precut edges, you only need to make two more cuts. Better yet, have the tabletop cut to exactly 36" square at your home center. It's free, and they can do a better job than most of us can.

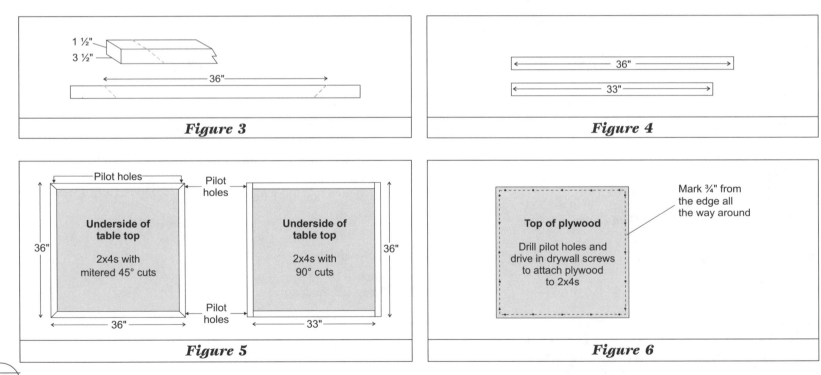

1 ½"
3 ½"
36"

Figure 3

36"
33"

Figure 4

Pilot holes
Pilot holes

Underside of table top

36"

2x4s with mitered 45° cuts

36"

Underside of table top

36"

2x4s with 90° cuts

Pilot holes

33"

Figure 5

Top of plywood

Drill pilot holes and drive in drywall screws to attach plywood to 2x4s

Mark ¾" from the edge all the way around

Figure 6

2. Most circular saws and all table saws can be set to cut at a 45° angle (see Figure 1). Set your saw for this angle and cut four pieces 36" long as shown in Figures 2 and 3. These are the sides for the table top.

   NOTE: If your saw is only able to cut at 90°, cut two 36" long pieces and two 33" long pieces as shown in Figure 4.

3. Determine which side of the plywood is the "D" side (the rougher, unfinished side), then place the plywood on a flat surface with the D side facing *up*. Line up the 2x4s you have cut so that they are flush with the sides of the plywood as shown in Figure 5. Drill pilot holes in one corner of the 2x4 assembly as illustrated and then drive in 3" drywall screws. For mitered corners (45° angles), use two screws and be sure to stagger them so that they don't hit each other. If you made 90° cuts in step 2, use one screw per corner. Repeat for each of the other three corners.

   NOTE: If the corners are mitered, they may not match exactly. Don't worry, you can put caulk in any gaps in step 6.

5. Flip the plywood and 2x4 assembly so that the 2x4s are underneath and the plywood is on top. Be careful not to twist or damage the 2x4 assembly as you do this. Measure ³/₄" from the edge of each side of the table top and mark lines all the way around as shown in Figure 6. Using these lines as a guide, drill five to seven pilot holes per side and then drive in 2" long drywall screws.

6. (Optional) Caulk the seams where the 2x4s meet the plywood. This will make painting and cleaning easier and cover any mistakes you might have made.

7. Apply a coat of primer to the table top. Start from the underside. When this is dry, turn the table top over. Apply a primer coat to the top surface of the table. Immediately, before the surface starts to dry, sprinkle play sand through a kitchen strainer from a height of about 8" to 12". You are trying to get a light, even dusting of fine sand over the *entire* top surface. It's better to apply too much sand than too little; the excess will shake off after the paint dries.

8. When the paint is dry, invert the table top and let the loose sand fall away. Apply the final coat of paint in the color of your choosing.

Making the PVC Table Base

While the paint is drying on the table top, assemble the table base.

1. Cut eight 27" pieces of PVC.

2. Make the top of the table base by assembling four of the 27" pieces into a square as shown in Figure 7 and connecting them with four 3-way ells. Do *not* glue yet! Make another identical assembly to form the bottom of the table base. Don't glue this assembly either.

3. Double-check that both assemblies are exactly the same size and that they fit into the space formed by the 2x4s under the table top. If they're too large, trim the PVC pipe the same amount on all eight pieces to make the square a bit smaller. Working on a flat surface, cement the top assembly together. Repeat for the bottom assembly.

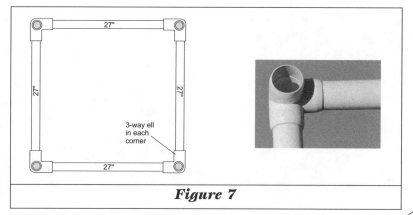

Figure 7

table and weaves

4. Cut the legs for your table from the remaining 1 ¹/₂" PVC pipe. The following chart shows the length the table legs need to be for each regulation table height. Cut *four* legs of the specified length for each table height you want.

Organization	Table Height	Length of Legs
AKC	8"	2"
	16"	10"
	24"	18"
USDAA	12"	6"
	16"	10"
	24"	18"

5. Figure 8 shows the top and bottom parts of the PVC table base with one set of legs, and Figure 9 shows what the base looks like assembled. If you want the table to be a single, permanent height, glue the legs into the top frame, then spread glue on all the bottom joints and slide the bottom frame onto the four legs. If you want an adjustable table, simply assemble the base in the same way without any glue. It will be quite steady if all the joints are square and the PVC legs are tightly pushed into the top and bottom frames.

Final Assembly

Once the paint on the table top is dry, simply set the table top onto the PVC base as shown in Figure 10. Gravity will do the rest.

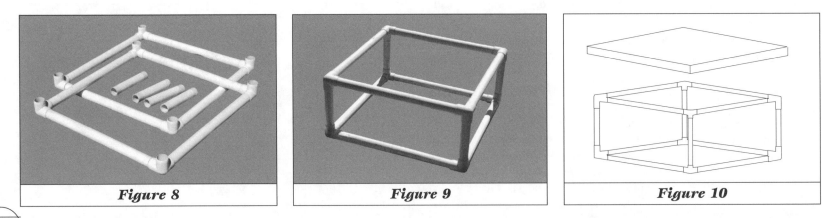

Figure 8   **Figure 9**   **Figure 10**

$\mathcal{S}$imple indoor/outdoor weave poles

the weave pole bases in these plans are suitable for use indoors or outdoors and can be made to accommodate 10 or 12 poles. Although they are technically legal for competition, they are intended primarily for classes or backyard training. If you need a set of weave poles able to hold up to the abuse of trials, make the weave poles with pipe flanges in the next set of plans. In training, it's a good idea to vary the number of weave poles wherever possible. By building five sets of six-pole bases (using the 10' boards), you can even practice 30 weave pole challenges.

Making the Bases

The number of end caps and PVC adapters and the length of lumber you get depends on how many poles you want to have in a set.

Materials Needed

To make 10 poles (two sets of five), buy the following:

- 10 – 1" schedule 40 PVC end caps

  NOTE: Get the kind with flat tops, not the domed tops.

- 10 – $^3/_4$" PVC adapters

  NOTE: These are cylinders with an outer diameter of 1 $^1/_4$" so they should fit snugly inside the 1" caps you are buying. If not, try another store.

- 2 – 1" x 4" x 8' fir or pine boards

To make 12 poles (two sets of six), buy the following:

- 12 – 1" schedule 40 PVC end caps
- 12 – $^3/_4$" PVC adapters
- 2 – 1" x 4" x 10' fir or pine boards

Regardless of whether you're making a set of 10 poles or a set of 12, buy:

- 4 – 24" aluminum bars, $^1/_8$" thick and 1" to 1 $^1/_2$" wide

  NOTE: If can't find these, order #E-ZRTA-2/16-24 from Small Parts.

- 24 – 8-32 x 1 $^1/_2$" flathead machine screws
- 8 – 8-32 x 1" flathead machine screws
- 32 – 8-32 nuts for machine screws
- 32 – #8 split lock washers
- Paint (if bases are to be used outdoors)
- PVC cement

Tools Needed

- Drill with $^3/_{32}$", $^3/_{16}$", and $^7/_{32}$" bits, countersink, and flat and Phillips head screwdriver bits
- C-clamps or spring clamps
- Socket set (preferably deep socket) with an $^{11}/_{32}$" socket (a wrench or pair of pliers will do if necessary)
- Hacksaw or Dremel tool with cutoff wheel
- Carpenter's ruler or tape measure
- Pencil or marker

Directions

1. At each end of one of the boards, mark the center of its width using a carpenter's ruler or tape measure—the board is 3 $\frac{1}{2}$" wide so the marks will be 1 $\frac{3}{4}$" from the edge. Using the second board as a guide, draw a line through these marks. Repeat for the second board.

2. Measuring from the end of the board, make a mark across the center line at 10" and then make a mark every 20" (at 30", 50", and so on) until you can't make another mark. Repeat for the other board.

   NOTE: For the 10-pole set, there will be 6" left at one end of each board. When you put the two boards together, you will have to make sure the 6" gaps are at opposite ends of the set so that the 20" pole spacing is correct. For the 12-pole set, there will be 10" left at the end of each board so it won't matter which ends of the boards are placed together.

3. If the aluminum bar you purchased is longer than 24", use a hacksaw or Dremel tool to cut it so that you have four 24" long pieces. Wear goggles! These bars will serve as stabilizers to keep the weave poles from tipping over.

4. Clamp a 24" bar on the unmarked side of the board. Position the bar flush with the end of the board and measure to make sure it is centered. Using the $\frac{3}{32}$" bit, drill two holes going through the alumi-num and the wood. Drill through the same holes with the $\frac{7}{32}$" bit to enlarge them. Use the countersink to make room for the heads of the machine screws so that they do not protrude from the bar. Attach the aluminum bar to the base using two 8-32 x 1" machine screws and 8-32 nuts as shown in Figures 1 and 2. Repeat for the other end of the board and for the second board.

5. Turn the boards over so that you can see the marks you made previously. Hold a PVC cap with the open end toward you and drill two $\frac{3}{16}$" holes through the cap and the wood as shown in Figure 3. (The holes should be far enough apart that the nuts you add in the next step can be turned freely without interfering with each other or with the walls of the cap.) Repeat this process for each of the five or six marks on each board. Turn the boards over and drill countersink holes in each of the drill holes.

6. Attach each PVC cap to the board. Insert a machine screw in each hole (two per cap) and then add a lock washer and a nut as shown in Figure 4. Tighten (very tight) using a screwdriver and socket set. Repeat for each of the 10 or 12 end caps.

7. Coat a $\frac{3}{4}$" PVC adapter with cement and push it into place inside the end cap on the board as shown in Figure 5. This should be a tight fit. Repeat for each of the 10 or 12 end caps.

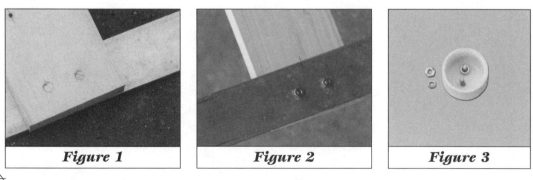

Figure 1   **Figure 2**   **Figure 3**

table and weaves

Making the Poles

These poles are easy to make and fit in the bases described in the previous section.

Materials Needed

- 4 – 10' lengths ³/₄" schedule 40 PVC
- 12 – ³/₄" schedule 40 PVC end caps
- PVC cement

Tools Needed

- Hacksaw or scissors-type PVC cutting shears
- Carpenter's ruler or tape measure

Directions

1. Make two marks on each length of PVC, measuring 40" from each end. These marks will be 40" apart so that you'll get three weave poles from each 10' long piece of pipe.
2. Cut the PVC into 40" lengths using the PVC shears or hacksaw.
3. Glue an end cap on one end of each of the cut poles.
4. Insert the uncapped end of each pole into one of the caps on your bases.

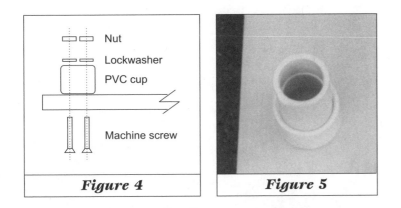

Nut

Lockwasher

PVC cup

Machine screw

Figure 4

Figure 5

table and weaves

*i*ndoor/outdoor weave poles for competition

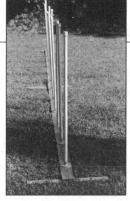

these plans are for making two sets of six weave poles with 22" spacing. You might consider making a set of two, three, or four weave poles in addition to these two sets of six so that you can set up any number of weave poles from 8 to 16 for practice or trials.

To make a set of two weave poles, cut a board to 44"; to make a set of three weave poles, cut a board to 66"; and to make a set of four, cut a board to 88". All other instructions are the same. Don't forget to adjust your shopping list for the right number of plumbing parts and get two extra lengths of 10' PVC so that you'll have enough poles. Each 10' long piece of PVC makes three poles.

Retrofitting Spring-Based Poles

This design is essentially the same as the flexible, spring-based weave poles that were featured in *Clean Run* magazine V7, #6 (June 2001). If you made the poles in that article or similar spring poles and want to retrofit them to comply with the new AKC regulations, purchase twelve $^1/_2$" x $^3/_8$" bushings and twelve $^3/_8$" pipe nipples. Then, strip your weave poles down to the floor flanges; that is, remove the springs (saying good-bye to $100 in the process) and $^1/_2$" pipe nipples. If your poles are rusted out (as mine were), you may also have to replace some or all of the $^1/_2$" floor flanges. Screw a bushing into each floor flange and add a $^3/_8$" pipe nipple to each flange/bushing assembly. Slip the $^3/_4$" PVC pole over the pipe nipple and you are ready to go.

Making the Bases

Materials Needed

- 2 – 1" x 4" x 12' fir or pine boards
- 12 – $^1/_2$" galvanized floor flanges
- 12 – $^1/_2$" x $^3/_8$" galvanized bushings
- 12 – $^3/_8$" x 4" galvanized pipe nipples, threaded at both ends

  NOTE: Check the photos to make sure that you select the correct flanges and bushings. Then, before you leave the store, make sure that the floor flanges, bushings, and nipples (in that order) all fit together. It's common to find mismatches when the parts in the bins get mixed up.

- 4 – $^1/_8$" thick x 1" to 1 $^1/_2$" wide x 24" aluminum bars

  NOTE: If you have difficulty finding these, order part #E-ZRTA-2/16-24 from Small Parts Inc.

- 48 – #10 x $^3/_4$" flat-head wood screws
- 8 – 8-32 x 1" flat-head machine screws
- 8 – 8-32 nuts for machine screws
- 8 – #8 split-lock washers
- Paint
- 8 – $^1/_4$" x 3" hex head lag screws (see step 6 to decide if you are going to need these for stakes)

Tools Needed

- Drill with $^3/_{32}$", $^3/_{16}$", and $^7/_{32}$" bits, countersink, and flat and Phillips head screwdriver bits
- C-clamps or spring clamps
- Socket set (preferably a deep socket set) with an $^{11}/_{32}$" socket (if you don't have this, a wrench or pliers will do in a pinch)
- Circular saw, table saw, miter saw, or crosscut saw
- Hacksaw or Dremel tool with cutoff wheel
- Carpenter's ruler or tape measure
- Pencil or marker

Directions

1. Cut each board to a length of 132" (11').
2. At each end of one of the boards, mark the center of its width using a carpenter's ruler or tape measure—the board is 3 $^1/_2$" wide so the marks will be 1 $^3/_4$" from the edge. Using the second board as a guide, draw a line through these marks. Repeat for the second board.
3. Measuring from the end of the board, make a mark across the center line at 11" and then make a mark every 22" (at 33", 55", and so on) until you can't make another mark. Repeat for the other board.

4. If the aluminum bar you purchased is longer than 24", use a hacksaw or Dremel tool to cut it so that you have four 24" long pieces. Wear goggles! These bars will serve as stabilizers to keep the weave poles from tipping over.
5. Clamp a 24" bar on the unmarked side of the board. Position the bar flush with the end of the board and measure to make sure it is centered. Using the $^3/_{32}$" bit, drill two holes going through the aluminum and the wood. Drill through the same holes with the $^7/_{32}$" bit to enlarge them. Use the countersink to make room for the heads of the machine screws so that they do not protrude from the bar. Attach the aluminum bar to the base using two 8-32 x 1" machine screws and 8-32 nuts as shown in Figures 1 and 2. Repeat for the other end of the board and for the second board.
6. The regulations require that the weave pole bases be fixed in place on the running surface. On carpet or mats, you can use duct tape or gaffer's tape to secure the weave poles. On dirt or grass, you'll need to use four $^1/_4$" x 3" hex head lag screws to secure each base. Drill a $^9/_{32}$" hole about 1" from the end of each stabilizer bar. The lag screws will be drilled into the ground through these holes. (A reversible cordless electric drill is highly recommended for this task, but a socket wrench can be used in a pinch.)

Figure 1

Figure 2

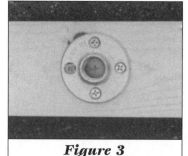

Figure 3

Figure 4

table and weaves

7. Turn the boards over so that you can see the marks you made previously. Center a floor flange on each of the marks, then drill pilot holes (four in all) for each flange. Using the electric screwdriver, drive a #10 x $^3/_4$" wood screw through the holes in the flange into the wood as shown in Figure 3. Repeat for all 12 floor flanges.

8. Screw a $^1/_2$" x $^3/_8$" galvanized bushing into each floor flange and then screw a $^3/_8$" x 4" pipe nipple into each galvanized bushing as shown in Figure 4.

9. Paint the bases.

Making the Poles

Materials Needed
- 4 – 10' lengths $^3/_4$" schedule 40 PVC
- 12 – $^3/_4$" PVC end caps
- PVC cement

Tools Needed
- Hacksaw or scissors-type PVC cutting shears
- Carpenter's ruler or tape measure

Directions
1. Make two marks on each length of PVC pipe, measuring 40" from each end. These marks will be 40" apart so that you'll get three weave poles from each 10' long piece of pipe.

2. Cut the PVC into 40" lengths using the shears or hacksaw.

3. Glue an end cap on one end of each of the cut poles. Set aside to dry.

4. Slip the open end of each PVC pole onto a $^3/_8$" pipe nipple.

table and weaves

table and weaves

*t*raining weave poles

most trainers would agree that of all the obstacles, the weave poles are the hardest to teach the dog since there are so many aspects involved in the performance (such as proper entry, the weaving motion, and staying in the entire set). The best way to train the weave poles is to create a pattern of movement that will be stored in a part of the dog's brain called the cerebellum. This is called "muscle memory" even though it's the brain that gets modified and it's the brain where the memories are stored. To create muscle memory, repetition is important. Just be careful not to repeat until the point of boredom or injury. Young dogs with their soft spines and gooey intervertebral disks (the cushioning pads between vertebrae in the spinal column) are the most susceptible to injury. This shows up as a repetitive stress syndrome, something like carpal tunnel syndrome in people.

There are several different types of training weaves that you can set up. Which one is best? That's a good way to start a fistfight in an agility barroom. Some dogs take to one or the other better, so it's always good to have different types of training devices around.

These plans are for making a base for training with staggered weave poles as shown in Figure 1. You can slide the two rows of weave poles closer together as the dog learns. There are also instructions included for modifying the poles themselves so that they have guide "wires" (in this case, rigid plastic tubing) as shown in Figure 2.

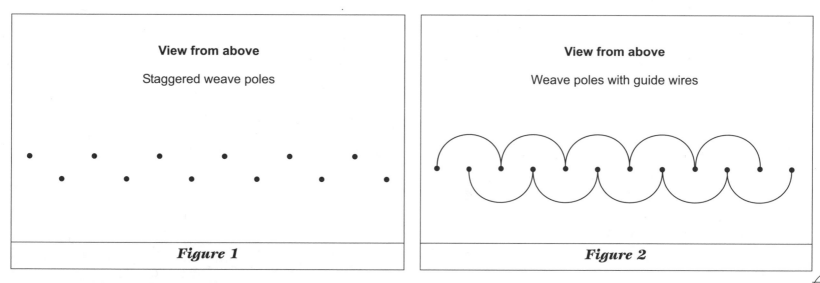

View from above	**View from above**
Staggered weave poles	Weave poles with guide wires
Figure 1	*Figure 2*

table and weaves

Making the Bases

Materials Needed

- 4 – 10' lengths $^3/_4$" schedule 40 PVC
- 1 – 10' length $^1/_2$" schedule 40 PVC
- 16 – $^3/_4$" PVC tees
- 4 – $^1/_2$" PVC end caps
- PVC cement
- (Optional) 4 – 10' lengths $^1/_2$" schedule 40 PVC pipe or 40' of electrical conduit which will fit inside $^3/_4$" PVC tees (see step 5 to see if you will need this)

Tools Needed

- Scissors-type PVC cutting shears
- Carpenter's ruler or tape measure
- Pencil or marker
- Hacksaw or Dremel tool (if conduit is used)

Directions

1. Cut the following pieces from the $^3/_4$" PVC:

   10 – 40" long
   2 – 10" long
   2 – 30" long

2. Glue a $^3/_4$" tee onto *one* end of each 10" and 30" long piece as shown in Figure 3.

3. Find a clean, flat place (like a driveway or patio) suitable for assembling a base that is going to be 20' long.

4. Collect five 40" pieces of $^3/_4$" PVC, a 10" piece of $^3/_4$" PVC with the tee you glued on, a 30" piece of $^3/_4$" PVC with the tee you glued on, and six $^3/_4$" tees. Start with the 10" piece with the tee attached. Glue a tee onto the opposite end of this assembly, making sure that the open mouth of the tee points straight up in the air as shown in Figure 4. (You can insert a scrap piece of PVC in the open mouth of the tee so that you can easily see if the tee is rotated even slightly.) Add a 40" piece of PVC and then another tee. Keep this going, alternating 40" pieces and tees, until you have added six tees with their open ends facing up (this is where you will insert the weave poles).

5. (Optional) If you are worried that the base is too floppy or bends in the middle, you can stiffen it by inserting 20' of electrical conduit (in a single piece if you can get it) or two 10' pieces of $^1/_2$" PVC. Trim the conduit or PVC, if necessary, with a hacksaw or Dremel tool so that no more than 30" sticks out at the open end of the base.

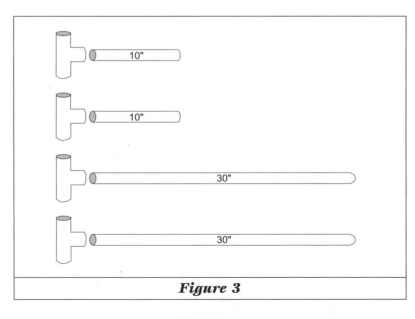

Figure 3

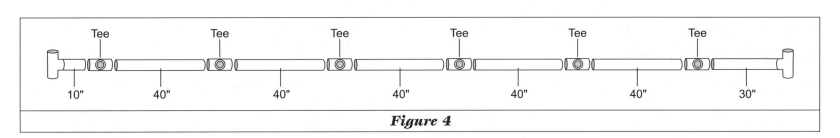

Figure 4

6. Finish the base by gluing the 30" piece with the tee attached to the last tee you glued on in step 4.

7. Repeat steps 4-6 to make the other base. The bases should be identical.

8. Set up the bases, side by side, so that the 30" piece on the end of one base is next to, and parallel with, the 10" piece on the end of the other base. This will give you two lines of weave poles, slightly staggered, with 20" spacing between poles as shown in Figure 5.

9. Cut two 30" pieces from the ½" PVC. (You will have 60" left over for other projects.) Slide a piece through the end tees in each base so that you connect the bases as shown in Figure 5. Check to make sure all is well, then glue end caps on the ½" PVC to keep the sliding base assemblies in place.

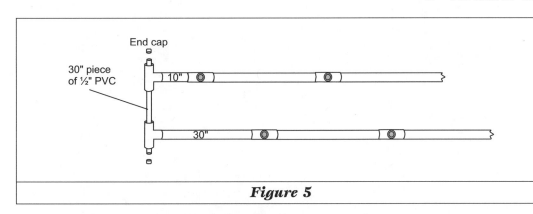

Figure 5

Making Weave Poles Without Wires

If you do not want poles with guidewires, follow the directions in this section. If you do want guidewires, proceed to the next section to make the poles for your bases.

Materials Needed

- 4 – 10' lengths ³/₄" schedule 40 PVC
- 12 – ³/₄" PVC end caps

Directions

1. Cut each 10' length (120") of ³/₄" PVC into thirds (that is, three pieces that are each 40" long). These will be your 12 weave poles.

2. Insert a pole into each of the open tees on the bases.

3. Glue a ³/₄" end cap onto each of the 12 poles.

TIP: If you will be using these weave poles for classes, or if you need to keep your dog on-lead while using the training poles, buy additional PVC and make a set of "shortie" weave poles that are only about 24" high.

Making Weave Poles with Guidewires: Type 1

There are two ways to make the special fittings you need to hold the guidewires for the poles. The first, which I call "Type 1," is preferred; it's cheaper and the parts are easier to work with. However, if you can't find the material you need for the plans below, then go with Type 2.

Materials Needed

- 4 – 10' lengths ³/₄" schedule 40 PVC
- 20 – ³/₄" PVC tees with one threaded joint and two slip-fitting joints
- 20 – ³/₄" threaded to ¹/₂" barbed hose fitting reducing adapters

NOTE: Figure 6 shows the two preceding parts connected together. The white fitting is the tee and the black fitting is the reducing adapter.

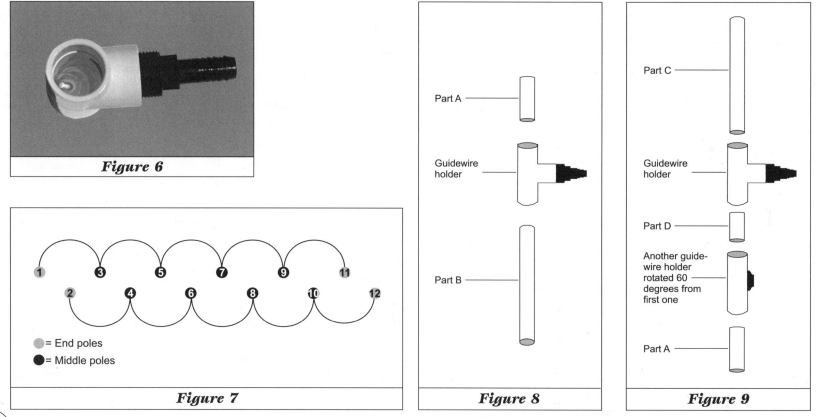

Figure 6

Figure 7

Part A
Guidewire holder
Part B

Figure 8

Part C
Guidewire holder
Part D
Another guide-wire holder rotated 60 degrees from first one
Part A

Figure 9

= End poles
= Middle poles

table and weaves

- 12 – ³/₄" PVC end caps
- 2 – 25' rolls polybutylene tubing

  NOTE: This is gray in color and fairly stiff, which keeps it from sagging over a span of more than 40". It's also expensive; plan to spend about $50 for the tubing alone. This tubing probably won't be available in a home center; try a local plumbing supply. If all else fails, try http://catalog.plumbshop.com/.

- PVC cement

Tools Needed

- Scissors-type PVC cutting shears
- Carpenter's ruler or tape measure
- Pencil or marker

Directions

1. Make the guidewire holders. Screw a ³/₄" threaded to ¹/₂" barbed hose fitting reducing adapter into the threaded joint of a ³/₄" PVC tee as shown in Figure 6. Make 20 of these assemblies.

2. You need to customize the height of the guides so that they are visible to *your* dog. With your dog standing, measure from the ground to your dog's eye level and write down this measurement. You don't need to be incredibly accurate, just within a few inches.

3. Cut 12 part As from the ³/₄" PVC. To determine the length for part A, subtract 1" from the measurement you got in step 2. For example, if eye level for your dog is 12", cut 12 pieces of PVC that are 11" long (12" – 1" = 11").

4. Cut 4 part Bs from the ³/₄" PVC. To determine the length for part B, subtract the measurement you got in step 2 from 40". For example, if eye level for your dog is 12", cut 4 pieces of PVC that are 28" long (40" – 12" = 28").

5. Cut 8 part Cs from the ³/₄" PVC. To determine the length for part C, subtract the measurement you got in step 2 from 37". For example, if eye level for your dog is 12", cut 8 pieces of PVC that are 25" long (37" – 12" = 25").

6. Cut 8 part Ds from the ³/₄" PVC. Part D is 2" long for all dogs.

7. Make four weave poles for the ends of the bases (see Figure 7). Collect four part A pieces of PVC, four part B pieces of PVC, and four guidewire holders. Glue one part A into one end of the tee of a guidewire holder, and glue one part B into the other end as shown in Figure 8. Repeat to make three more poles.

8. Make eight middle poles (see Figure 7). Collect 8 part A pieces of PVC, 8 part C pieces of PVC, 8 part D pieces of PVC, and 16 guidewire holders. Glue one part C into one end of the tee of a guidewire holder, and glue one part D into the other end. Take a second guidewire holder, and glue it onto the other end of part D, rotating it to about 60° from the first one as shown in Figures 9 and 10. You can lay the pole on top of the drawing in Figure 10 to guide you. You may want to position the pieces without gluing, make a mark to guide you, and then glue. Finish the weave pole with a part A. Repeat to make seven more poles.

9. Determine which end is "up" on each pole; the longer piece of PVC on each will be at the top of the pole for most dogs (except the very largest). Glue an end cap onto the top of each.

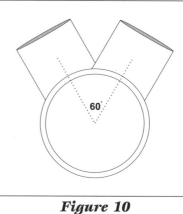

Figure 10

table and weaves

10. Place the weave poles in the bases you made so that the guidewire holders from the two end poles point in opposite directions (refer to Figure 7 as needed). Then, continue adding poles along the row, alternating the direction in which the guidewire holders point. The eight middle poles have two guidewire holders so that each one can hold two wires. Finally, the last two poles have one guidewire holder each, as at the beginning of the row.

11. Once you have the weave poles in place, hold the polybutylene tubing between pole #1 and pole #3 and mark where you want to make your cut to form a guide connecting these two poles. (The tubing comes in a coil; use the curve of the tubing to your advantage and try to match the curve between the two poles.) Cut the tubing with the shears or a sharp knife and use it to connect pole #1 to #3. Connect pole #2 to pole #4 in the same manner. Continue in this fashion until all the poles are connected. Make sure you have set things up so that the dog enters moving from right to left as it enters the poles.

Making Weave Poles with Guidewires: Type 2

If you couldn't find the right parts for making the Type 1 weave poles with guidewires, follow these instructions.

Materials Needed

- 4 – 10' lengths $^3/_4$" schedule 40 PVC
- 20 – $^3/_4$" PVC tees
- 20 – 1" schedule 40 PVC slip fitting to $^3/_4$" threaded fitting reducing adapters

  NOTE: See Figure 11 if you're not sure what this fitting looks like.
- 20 – $^1/_2$" x 3" carriage bolts

  NOTE: Make sure the head fits inside the reducing adapter.
- 20 – $^1/_2$" hex nuts
- 12 – $^3/_4$" PVC end caps
- 2 – 25' rolls polybutylene tubing

  NOTE: This is gray in color and fairly stiff, which keeps it from sagging over a span of more than 40". It's also expensive; plan to spend about $50 for the tubing alone. This tubing probably won't be available in a home center; try a local plumbing supply. If all else fails, try http://catalog.plumbshop.com/.
- PVC cement

Tools Needed

- Scissors-type PVC cutting shears
- Slip-jaw pliers or an adjustable wrench that fits the nuts you purchased
- Carpenter's ruler or tape measure
- Pencil or marker

Directions

Making the Type 2 guidewire holders takes more steps than for the Type 1 guidewire holders.

1. Feed a carriage bolt into the reducing adapter with the threads of the bolt protruding from the hole in the threaded end of the adapter as shown in Figure 12.

2. Screw a nut onto this carriage bolt to fix it in place. Tighten it with the pliers or wrench.

3. Glue the adapter/bolt/nut assembly onto the middle arm of the tee as shown in Figure 12.

4. Repeat steps 1-3 to make 19 more guide holder assemblies.

Once you have completed the guidewires holders, the instructions for making the poles are the same as for Type 1 poles. Follow steps 2 through 11 in the previous section.

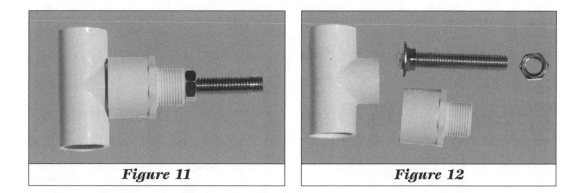

Figure 11   *Figure 12*

table and weaves

table and weaves